AMERICAN PIT BULL TERRIER

Jacqueline O'Neil

HOWELL
BOOK
HOUSE

Howell Book House
MACMILLAN
A Prentice Hall Macmillan Company
1633 Broadway
New York, NY 10019

Library of Congress Cataloging-in-Publication Data

O'Neil, Jacqueline.

The ultimate American pit bull terrier/Jacqueline O'Neil

p. cm.

ISBN: 0-87605-248-0

1.American pit bull terrier. I. Title

SF429.A72F735 1995

636.7'55—dc20 CIP

Manufactured in the United States of America

10 9 8 7 6 5 4 3 2 1

Book Design by Kris Tobiassen

To Tom O'Neil, a superior navigator

CONTENTS

FROM THE AUTHOR

The term "Pit Bull," when used in this book, is an abbreviation for "American Pit Bull Terrier," meaning a dog whose parents were both purebred American Pit Bull Terriers. In recent years, the media have misused the term *Pit Bull*, calling practically every dog that gets into trouble by that name—including all manner of mongrels and mixed-bred dogs. As a result, many American Pit Bull Terrier owners have stopped using their breed's traditional nickname. But that's simply not fair. We still call Doberman Pinschers "Dobes," Shetland Sheepdogs "Shelties" and Labrador Retrievers "Labs." The real American Pit Bull Terrier is not a culprit, but a victim, and deserves to keep its nickname the same as any other breed.

INTRODUCTION

Gary Watkins, eleven years old, was absorbed in chasing lizards when Weela, the family Pit Bull, plowed into him with a body slam that sent him sprawling. Gary's mother, Lori, saw the whole incident and remembers being surprised at first, because Weela always played kindly with children. But her surprise quickly turned to horror when she saw a rattlesnake sink its fangs into Weela's face. Somehow Weela had sensed the snake's presence from across the yard and rushed to push Gary out of striking range.

Luckily for thirty people, twenty-nine dogs, thirteen horses and a cat, Weela recovered from the snake's venom. Luckily, because that's how many lives she saved a few years later. For her heroism, Weela was named Ken-L Ration's Dog Hero of the Year in 1993. The press release read in part:

> In January 1993, heavy rains caused a dam to break miles upstream on the Tijuana River, normally a narrow, three-foot-wide river. Weela's rescue efforts began at a ranch that belonged to a friend of her owners, Lori and Daniel Watkins. Weela and the Watkinses worked for six hours battling heavy rains, strong currents and floating debris to reach the ranch and rescue their friend's twelve dogs.
>
> From that experience, the Watkinses recognized Weela's extraordinary ability to sense quicksand, dangerous drop-offs and mud bogs. "She was constantly willing to put herself in dangerous

situations," says Lori Watkins. "She always took the lead except to circle back if someone needed help."

Periodically, over a month's time, sixty-five-pound Weela crossed the flooded river to bring food to seventeen dogs and puppies and one cat, all stranded on an island. Each trip she pulled thirty to fifty pounds of dog food that had been loaded into a harnessed backpack. The animals were finally evacuated on Valentine's Day.

On another occasion, Weela led a rescue team to thirteen horses stranded on a large manure pile completely surrounded by floodwaters. The rescue team successfully brought the horses to safe ground.

Finally, during one of Weela's trips back from delivering food to stranded animals, she came upon a group of thirty people who were attempting to cross the floodwaters. Weela, by barking and running back and forth, refused to allow them to cross at that point where the waters ran deep and fast. She then led the group to a shallower crossing upstream, where they safely crossed to the other side.

The story of Weela's heroism appeared in *Good Housekeeping* magazine. Paul Harvey discussed her on his radio show. She was a guest of honor at Hollywood's prestigious Genesis Awards, and her picture and story graced the souvenir book.

Strong, gentle, intelligent and brave, Weela, CGC, TT, is the ultimate American Pit Bull Terrier, epitomizing the best that the breed has to offer. But her story also highlights an important yet often misunderstood fact about the breed. The Pit Bull is a dog that loves to please its owner and tries to become whatever kind of dog its owner desires. Weela has had two owners. The first owner dumped her in an alley to die when she was less than four weeks old. Her present owner, Lori Watkins, found five starving Pit Bull puppies whimpering in an alley, took them home and raised them. Later, the Watkins family placed four of the puppies in loving homes and kept the little female they named Weela. They believed Weela was special, and she proved them right. Most Pit Bull puppies grow up to become a reflection of both their owners' personality and the care and training they receive. One can only imagine what a different dog Weela would have become if her original owner had raised her, and she had done her best to please him.

The strongest dog in the world for its size, the American Pit Bull Terrier is confident and alert. Endowed with nearly human facial expressions, the breed's bright eyes and inquisitively wrinkled forehead make it both handsome and comical. With its muscular yet agile body, sleek coat and quick intelligence, the Pit Bull is a large dog compacted into a medium-sized bundle of energy—enough dog for anyone and too much dog for some.

Lori Watkins with Weela, Ken-L Ration's 1993 Dog Hero of the Year.

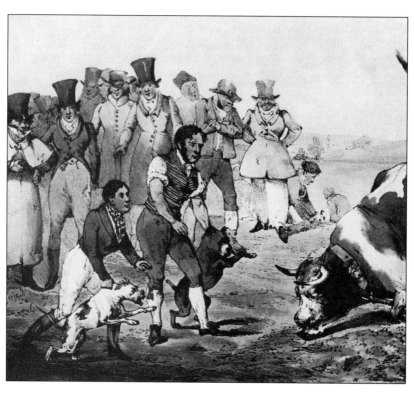

Bull-Fight: "If you go near, Master George, he will pink you." Henry Aiken, ca. 1820.

CHAPTER 1

The American Pit Bull Terrier, *Then*

Archeologists agree that dogs were the first animals domesticated by humans. Cave drawings from the Paleolithic era, the earliest part of the Old World Stone Age (some fifty thousand years ago), show men and dogs hunting together. Gradually, humans found additional uses for dogs. The earliest known ancestors of the American Pit Bull Terrier served as guards and draft animals, but they were especially esteemed as dogs of war.

ORIGIN OF THE PIT BULL

The ancient Greeks had huge, ferocious dogs of a type called Mollossian that historians believe originated in Asia. During the sixth century B.C., Phoenician traders brought some of these Greek guard dogs to England. There they flourished and became the ancestors of England's early Mastiff-type dogs.

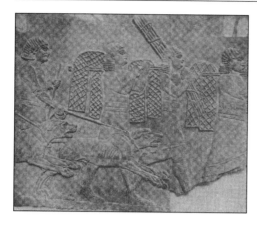

Picture of a bas-relief called Hunters with Nets and Mastiffs, from the walls of Assurbanipal's palace at Nineveh, 668–626 B.C. British Museum.

When the Roman legions invaded Britain, they were met on the beaches by the Britons' fierce Mastiff-type war dogs fighting side by side with their owners. The Romans admired these fighting dogs so much that they sent many of them home to Italy. There the dogs were called Pugnaces, or the broad-mouthed dogs of Britain. As the Roman legions and influence spread across Europe, so did the dogs.

Warrior dogs also starred in the bloody Roman circuses, where they were used to fight savage animals of other species, armed men and each other. In A.D. 395 , the Roman Claudian described "the British Hound that brings the bull's big forehead to the ground." His contemporary, the Roman historian Symmachus, wrote about seven Irish Bulldogs that excited a circus audience with their savage fighting and brave attitude. Symmachus called the deadly dogs Bulldogs, because dogs of that type were used to fight bulls.

The Ancient Bulldog

A Mastiff of true English blood
Lov'd fighting better than his food;
He glory'd in his limping pace,
The scars of honour seam'd his face;

In ev'ry limb a gash appears,
And frequent fights retrench'd his ears.

—Gay [from George R. Jesse's *Researches Into the History of the
British Dog* (London: R. Hardwicke, 1866)]

During ancient times there were no breeds as we know them today, and dogs were usually named for the work they did. For example, in England all guard dogs of massive size were considered Mastiffs, and all dogs quick, brave and small enough to enter a hole in the ground (terra) after wild game such as badger or fox were called terriers.

Eventually some of the Mastiff-type dogs became specialists. A 1632 dictionary defined the Alaunt as being like a Mastiff and serving the British butchers by rounding up and penning fierce oxen. The Bandog was any large guard dog that was kept chained by day. And the Bulldog, of course, was the gladiator.

George R. Jesse, the famed British canine historian, wrote that the Bulldog was the result of selectively breeding Mastiffs to produce a smaller, more agile dog with a recessed nose and a protruding jaw. This, Jesse contended, would enable the dog to breathe freely while holding onto a bull. He described the original Bulldog's appearance in *Researches Into the History of the British Dog*: "The lowering eye, somewhat projecting, the heavy jaw; broad, massive, round skull; distended nostrils, and in some cases teeth constantly exposed; together with his deep, ample, and muscular chest, gave this redoubted and formidable animal a terrific aspect not belied by his undaunted courage and invincible obstinacy in combat. He rarely barked or even growled, but attacked in silence and in front . . ."

The fearless, ferocious Bulldogs that were used to fight bulls and bears long ago were different than today's sophisticated "sourmugs" in both appearance and attitude. Ancient Bulldogs were taller and more agile, with nearly straight front legs, and they had longer muzzles than do modern Bulldogs. Some even had fairly long, straight tails.

THE BLOOD SPORTS

Blood sports were so much a part of daily life in old England that around 1800, in the town of Wednesbury in Staffordshire County, church bells rang in celebration of "Old Sal" when she finally managed to have puppies. Sal was famous for gameness but had not been able to whelp a litter before. If a Bulldog bitch died during whelping in that mining district, women often raised the puppies by suckling them at their own breasts.

Bullbaiting and other blood sports were not just entertainment for the working classes. In fact, kings and queens often mandated that a contest be arranged. When French ambassadors visited the court of Queen Elizabeth in 1559, the queen graciously entertained them with a fine dinner followed by an exhibition of dogs baiting bulls and bears. The ambassadors enjoyed it so much that they attended another baiting the following day. More than a quarter of a century later, the queen entertained the Danish ambassador the same way.

Bulldog, Sir Edwin Landseer, 1820.

Wasp, Schild and Billy, the Duke of Hamilton's Bulldogs, by H. B. Challon, 1809.

King James I continued Queen Elizabeth's tradition by having a special baiting arranged to entertain ambassadors from the Spanish court. The games included bulls, bears, horses and dogs, and, for the finale, a white bear was thrown into the Thames River and dogs baited it swimming. The first recorded prohibition of blood sports is also attributed to King James I. In 1618, he forbade them on Sundays for the sake of religion.

James I appointed Edward Alleyn to the position of Master of the King's Games of Bears, Bulls and Dogs. For Alleyn this was a second career. He was also an actor, ranked as one of the best, and was especially famous for his roles in Christopher Marlowe's plays. Alleyn founded Dulwich College and funded it with money partially earned from organizing and promoting bull- and bearbaiting.

King Charles I, James's son, was also an avid spectator of blood sports, and during the days of Queen Anne (1665–1714), such spectacles continued to flourish. A public advertisement during that period read:

At the Bear Garden in Hockley in the Hole, near Clerkenwell Green, this present Monday, there is a great match to be fought by two Dogs of Smithfield Bars against two Dogs of Hampstead, at the Reading Bull, for one guinea to be spent; five lets go out of hand; which goes fairest and farthest in wins all. The famous Bull of fireworks, which pleased the gentry to admiration. Likewise there are two Bear-Dogs to jump three jumps apiece at the Bear, which jumps highest for ten shillings to be spent. Also variety of Bull-baiting and Bear-baiting; it being a day of general sport by all the old gamesters; and a bull-dog to be drawn with fireworks. Beginning at three o'clock.

Bullbaiting

Evidence of bullbaiting's popularity in England centuries ago is still visible today. The old bull ring still stands in a few British towns. Some streets, especially in Dorchester and Birmingham, have names that refer to their proximity to the baiting ring. In fact, baiting was so established that some towns used to have a law forbidding butchers to sell bull meat unless the bull had been baited by dogs before it was slaughtered. The reason behind the ruling was the belief that meat from a baited bull was more tender and nutritious.

In at least one instance, bullbaiting was established in the name of charity. In 1661 a gentleman named George Staverton donated money to be used once a year to buy a bull to be baited at Wokingham. He stipulated that the flesh, hide and organ meat be sold and the money used to buy shoes and stockings for needy children. The Wokingham baiting was held yearly until 1823.

Before a baiting, the bull was prepared in a prescribed manner. Either a heavy rope was tied around its horns or a wide leather collar was buckled around its neck. A stake was driven into the ground and a large iron ring, acting as a swivel, was connected to it. Then one end of a heavy chain or rope was attached to the ring and the other end was fastened to the bull.

When a dog was released, it was expected to pin the bull by attacking it from the front and gripping its tender nose. Sometimes two or more dogs were released at the same time. Most bulls were tortured for hours in this manner before they were either killed by the dogs or slaughtered for meat, but an occasional bull became famous for its ability to defend itself and was used over and over. One of the best known was Bill Gibbons's bull, and he drew enormous crowds. Experienced and wise, as

Bull Broke Loose, Inbekannter Kunstler, London, 1821.

soon as he was attached to the ring he used his heavy hoofs to dig a hole. Then he protected his tender nose by burying it in the hole and met the dogs with hoofs and horns ready.

Few baited bulls fared so well. Attacked by multiple dogs, some tried to lay down in exhaustion, but fires were lighted under them to force them back on their feet. Tired or slow bulls often had their tails twisted until they broke and were poked in the tender parts with sharply pointed spikes to speed them up. In 1801, at Bury St. Edmonds, a bull's hoofs were hacked off, leaving the bull to defend itself on bloody stumps. A historian chronicled that event, but no one knows how many times such atrocities occurred.

For Bulldog owners, baiting was a compelling competitive event. They paid an entry fee for their dog to have a turn at the bull, and the owner of the dog that managed to pin the bull won a prize. During a baiting, bulls often tossed dogs thirty or more feet into the air. Meanwhile owners scrambled to line themselves up below their plummeting dog, hoping to break its fall by catching it on their own shoulders. Men sometimes got too close to the maddened bull and were also tossed. Dogs that were so deeply gored that their organs hung out were still urged by their owners to continue the assault, and many dauntless dogs were trampled under the bull's hoofs.

Written history about bullbaiting includes the story of a butcher who entered his elderly bitch at a baiting and brought along a litter of her puppies to sell. The reliable old bitch pinned the bull, but that wasn't enough for the butcher. While the bitch faithfully held the bull, he cut her to pieces with his cleaver. Since the bitch didn't quit her hold until she bled to death, the butcher achieved his purpose. The audience was so impressed with the bitch's gameness that her puppies were all sold on the spot and brought an excellent price.

Bearbaiting

Bearbaiting was similar to bullbaiting except that the bear's weapons were teeth and claws instead of horns and hoofs. Reports before the sixteenth century describe the bear wearing a collar and fastened to a ring and stake in the same manner as the bull. Later writings refer to a ring in the bear's nose.

Bearbaiting is thought to have been introduced into England by the Romans. During its heyday bearbaiting was the most popular diversion in the country.

Like exceptional bulls, an occasional bear became famous for its ferocity and fighting ability. Sackerson, an especially savage specimen, was mentioned by Shakespeare in *The Merry Wives of Windsor*.

As popular as blood sports were, not everyone approved:

What folly is this to keep with danger
A great mastiff dog and foul ugly bear
And to this anent, to see them two fight
With terrible tearings, a full ugly sight.

—Robert Crowley, (1518–88)

Dog and Lion Fights

Considered spectacular shows, and held much less frequently than either bear- or bullbaitings, dog and lion fights took place with the lion in a barred cage with spaces between the bars wide enough so a dog could be pushed through. An incident at Warwick in 1825 marked the end of these spectacles.

The lion at Warwick was Nero, a large, noble and rather docile male that feared no animal and fought only in self-defense. The three dogs shoved into his cage were described as a dog named Tiger, a fallow-colored dog, and a brown Bulldog named Turk. At only thirty-six pounds, Turk was much smaller than the other two, and his head was still swollen and raw from winning an earlier match against a much larger dog.

At the five-minutes mark, the fallow dog was so maimed it was considered useless and removed from the cage. Two minutes later, Tiger crawled out, gravely wounded. Turk continued to attack, pinning Nero's sensitive nose again and again, while the lion used his deadly claws to break each hold. Finally Nero had enough and held the profusely bleeding dog between his huge paws for more than a minute. He could have easily killed Turk with his teeth, but chose to simply hold him still so he couldn't attack.

Turk had fought Nero for eleven minutes when the cheering spectators slowly quieted and then began shouting to the gamekeepers to take the dog from the cage and spare his life. The gamekeepers tried, but Turk broke away from them and bled to death while charging at Nero one last time. The audience filed out, some silently and some in whispers, apparently embarrassed that their cries to stop the fight came too late to save the courageous little dog.

Dogfights

England passed the Humane Acts in 1835, making blood sports illegal. Although dogfighting was popular before then, it was often just one part of a full day of blood sports; a kind of warm-up before the main event. Interest in dogfighting grew rapidly after blood sports were abolished because, unlike bullbaiting rings, dogfighting pits didn't require much space. Contests could be secretly held in cellars and the back rooms of pubs.

In the United States, one of the most famous dog shows is called the Westminster Kennel Club show, or simply Westminster. Held at Madison Square Garden in New York City, and televised and reported around the world, this prestigious show is the second oldest annual sporting event in the United States. Only the Kentucky Derby is older.

In England, less than two centuries ago, the name Westminster was also well known for dogs. It was one of the largest and finest dogfighting pits in the country. Before the Humane Acts, dogfights at Westminster were a gala spectacle, as illustrated by this report from an 1825 issue of *The Sporting Magazine:*

> The Westminster Pit was crowded on Tuesday evening, January 18, with all the dog-fanciers in the metropolis, to witness a battle between the celebrated dog Boney and a black novice called Gas, lately introduced to the fancy by Charley, to whom the dog belongs. The stakes were forty sovereigns, and everything was arranged to the satisfaction of the amateurs. The pit was lighted with an elegant chandelier, and a profusion of waxlights. The dogs were brought to the scratch at eight o'clock in excellent condition, and were seconded by their respective masters. Boney was the

Dogfighting at the Westminster Pit, from a colored engraving, artist unknown, ca. 1820.

favourite at three to one, and so continued till within ten minutes of the termination of the contest—a confidence arising solely from his known bottom; for to the impartial spectator, Gas took the lead throughout. The battle lasted an hour and fifty minutes, when Boney was carried out insensible. He was immediately bled and put in a warm bath. There were nearly three hundred persons present.

As dogfighting's popularity soared, the contests became more organized. Fight rules were written and upheld and handlers developed conditioning programs (keeps) for their dogs in an effort to have them reach optimum fighting weight just before a match. A dog was said to be at its best fighting weight when it carried as few pounds as possible while maintaining its full strength. Much more than pride was involved in the desire to win. Betting was heavy and purses were large.

Gambling especially appealed to people who were so poor that only a stroke of luck could improve their living conditions. Many early dogfighters worked in dangerous trades and speculated on their own lives. For example, the miners of Staffordshire County, England, drew lots at the start of their shift to see who would work in the most hazardous locations. With frequent deaths from roof collapses, faulty machinery, gas fires and falls, daily survival was always a gamble for them. Worst of all, sometimes even hazardous work wasn't available. Three depressions in England between 1800 and 1850 made jobs so scarce that many people died of starvation. Between the depressions, periods of rapid industrial growth caused overcrowding and lack of sanitation. These were the decades of sweated labor in the major cities, and poor children were taken out of school by the age of ten and put to work for seventy-two-hour weeks.

As living conditions in the major British cities gradually improved, fewer people participated in dogfighting. But the horrid conditions in the industrial and mining counties to the north (as well as in parts of Ireland) lasted longer, prolonging the disregard for life that fed the blood sport mentality. People who gambled with their own lives had little to take pride in except a win with their fighting dog. Besides, the purse would provide money for food. It would hardly occur to them that fighting a dog might be cruel when their starving children worked beside them in the mines.

THE BULL AND TERRIER

During the early 1800s, some Bulldog breeders tried something new in hopes of breeding faster, fiercer fighters. They bred the most formidable baiting and fighting Bulldogs to the toughest, quickest and bravest Terriers. This cross was believed to enhance the fighting ability of the Bulldog by reducing its size, while maintaining its strength and increasing its speed and agility. Although some historians say the smooth-coated Black-and-Tan and the White English Terrier (now extinct) were most frequently crossed with Bulldogs, others say the terriers were chosen only on the basis of gameness and working ability, and a variety of terrier-like dogs were used. The result of these crosses was called the Bull and Terrier, or the Half-and-Half.

Although a few modern writers contend that today's Pit Bull is actually the original Bulldog as it appeared in the 1700s, without any crossbreeding with terriers, books and magazines from the period prove that the cross was made. By the early nineteenth century, when Bulldog-Terrier crosses became fashionable, dog books were also popular. In fact, more books and articles about dogs were published in that period than during all of the previous centuries combined, and many of these works discussed the results of the cross. For example, George R. Jesse wrote in *Researches Into the History of the British Dog*, published in London by R. Hardwicke in 1866, "The bull-terrier superseded the pure bulldog for the combats of the pit. The former, possessing much more quickness, consequently got the first hold, an important point, as all experienced fighters have a

Trusty, left, Lord Camelford's dog.

Dustman, right, another famous Bull and Terrier.

favourite place for attack." (*Researches Into the History of the British Dog*. London: R. Hardwicke, 1866)

An early Bull and Terrier named Trusty was so famous in England that an article and picture of him appeared in an 1806 edition of *The Sporting Magazine*. The picture is the first one known of a Bull and Terrier cross. Trusty was "as renowned for his battles as Bonaparte," according to the article, and "fought one hundred and four battles and was never beat." Raised by a prizefighter, and later owned by a succession of boxers, Trusty was eventually purchased by Lord Camelford and came to be known as Lord Camelford's dog. Later his lordship changed the dog's name to Belcher and presented him to fighting Jim Belcher, boxing champion of England. His Lordship explained that "the only unconquered man was the only fit master for the only unconquered dog."

The Sporting Magazine honored another Bull and Terrier in 1812. The article read, "Dustman is a celebrated dog . . . of a breed between a bull and a terrier. The breed of dogs of this description has been much encouraged of late, and is held in great estimation . . ."

Although they were both Bull and Terriers, Trusty and Dustman didn't resemble each other at all. Trusty looked like a small Bulldog, while Dustman appeared to be a stocky terrier. This was typical of the times. Before 1850, Bull and Terriers seldom resembled each other because people preferred choosing a Bulldog and a Terrier as breeding partners rather than breeding a Bull and Terrier to another Bull and Terrier. In 1832, for example, *The Sporting Magazine* honored Brutus by calling him a "celebrated bull Terrier . . . considered the perfect model of his kind . . . got by an English bull dog out of a small Irish Terrier."

Eventually people began breeding their best Bull and Terrier to another fine Bull and Terrier and, as time passed, Bull and Terriers became recognizable as an emerging breed. However, when reading nineteenth-century books or magazines, it's difficult to tell if a reference to a Bulldog means the original, straighter-legged British Bulldog, the more modern version of the Bulldog, a cross between a Bulldog and a Terrier or the result of breeding a Bull and Terrier to another Bull and Terrier. Many breeds were just developing at that time and were frequently mislabeled in literature, and illustrations captioned simply "Bull-dog" often resemble our modern Pit Bulls. Some of these were probably smallish, agile Bulldogs of the original, straighter-legged type, quick enough to be useful to a dogfighter. In fact, it's most likely that these lighter Bulldogs and the Bull and Terrier crosses were not only used for the same purposes, but were often bred to each other. It is their descendents that eventually fused into the Pit Bull.

Meanwhile, after 1860, living and working conditions improved for the miners, chainmakers and potters of England's industrial north and their Irish counterparts. Although gambling on dogs remained popular, blood sports such as dogfighting declined. In some areas, dog racing became the dominant sport, and Whippet races are still held today. In fact, the wretched, rugged and resolute laborers who modified their Bull and Terrier dogs until they perfected the world's most formidable canine fighting machine were the same people who conceived of and developed the Whippet.

ARRIVAL IN AMERICA

Blood sports were popular in America, too, and the first Bull-dogs and Bull and Terriers imported to the New World were brought over for that purpose. While bearbaiting was banned in

Young Storm and Old Storm, Bull and Terriers from The Sporting Magazine, London, 1824.

New England as early as the 1600s, public spectacles such as bullbaiting, rat-killing competitions for dogs, dogfighting and cockfighting were extremely popular in New York City during the late seventeenth and early eighteenth centuries. Nearly all of America's early fighting dogs were British or Irish imports bred for generations to do battle, and many of the Americans who imported them continued breeding for the same purpose.

Dogfighting was so accepted in America that in 1881, when a fight was held in Louisville between the famed English imports Lloyd's Pilot, owned by "Cockney Charlie" Lloyd, and Crib, owned by Louis Kreiger, the Ohio and Mississippi Railroad advertised special excursion fares to the big battle. Upon arrival in Louisville, bettors and spectators were taken to a fine hotel where they were warmly welcomed by the president of the Louisville board of aldermen, the police chief and other local officials. The referee for the fight was William Harding, sports editor of *The Police Gazette*; owner-publisher Richard K. Fox served as stakeholder. Pilot and Crib each weighed in at just under twenty-eight pounds and thrilled the spectators by fighting gamely for an hour and twenty-five minutes before Pilot won the victory.

"Cockney Charlie" Lloyd imported other dogs that gained fame fighting in America and were also used for breeding. Among them were Lloyd's Paddy, Pat and Rafferty. In fact, some of today's American Pit Bull Terrier owners can still trace their dog's ancestors back to several strains of superior fighting dogs that arrived in America during the 1800s. A few of these strains are Corvino, Delihant, Farmer, Feeley and Tudor from England; and Colby, Corcoran, Gas House, Lightner, Noonan and Semmes from Ireland. The designation "Old Family," still in use today, refers to the Irish dogs.

AMERICANIZATION OF THE BREED

Pilot and Crib, two of the most famous dogs of their period, weighed under twenty-eight pounds, yet the weight of a male Pit Bull today ranges between forty and sixty-five pounds. What happened? Yes, Pilot and Crib were at fighting weight. But while they normally would have weighed several pounds more, it wouldn't have been nearly enough to make up the difference.

One explanation is that Americans always seem to believe bigger is better, and selected bigger dogs for breeding until they created a larger animal. This account is partially true, but there is more to it than that.

It is believed that the breed's general usefulness on the frontier was a factor in increasing its size. The American pioneers discovered the Bull and Terriers' versatility, bravery and devotion, and soon the dogs traveled west, becoming indispensable members of many ranch and farm families. The dogs were well suited to life on the frontier, guarding homesteads and children with confidence and authority. Many of them also helped round up the stock. In addition, they protected the farm animals from predators and varmints, challenging everything from rats and snakes to coyotes and bears. Eventually the settlers decided a slightly larger dog with the same body style and bravery would have an even better chance when defending the stock against marauding mountain lions and ravaging wolves. Consequently, when selecting breeding partners for their dogs, they chose larger specimens.

While few of the pioneers kept breeding records on their dogs, American dogfighters painstakingly cataloged pedigrees of their breeding stock. In fact, they kept pedigrees, either in private files or in their heads, for generations. Many of them registered their dogs in 1898 when Chauncy Z. Bennett founded the United Kennel Club (UKC) with the American (Pit) Bull Terrier as its first recognized breed. Bennett created that breed name to help establish the dogs as an American breed, and registered his own dog, Bennett's Ring, as UKC No. 1. During its formative years, the UKC published its own dogfighting rules, but today its policy is against pitting dogs, and it will not knowingly accept advertisements from dogfighters.

The American Dog Breeders Association (ADBA) came into being in 1909 under the leadership of its first president, Guy McCord, and his close friend, John P. Colby. Originally dominated by breeders of fighting dogs, today it will not knowingly

World War I poster by Wallace Robinson. The Pit Bull in the middle represents the United States.

publish any material conflicting with the Animal Welfare Act of 1976. While some APBT breeders chose one organization or the other when registering their dogs, others listed their stock with both registries, and many still do.

THE DOG OF THE DAY

Every dog does not have its day, but the Pit Bull certainly did. Its day was just before and during World War I, when it was so highly regarded that it represented the United States on a World War I poster depicting each of the allied forces as a gallant dog native to its country. During that time, practically every issue of *Life* magazine featured political cartoons with Pit Bulls as the main characters. Pit Bulls even graced the covers of *Life* on February 4, 1915, and again on March 24, 1917. The first one, captioned "The Morning After," showed a bandaged and scarred Pit Bull; the latter, captioned "After Six," displayed a gentlemanly Pit Bull in a bow tie and top hat. Both were drawn by Will Rannells.

During World War I, the breed proved deserving of its country's esteem. A Pit Bull named Stubby was the war's most outstanding canine soldier. He earned the rank of sergeant, was mentioned in official dispatches and earned two medals. One was for warning of a gas attack and the other was for holding a German spy at Chemin des Dames until American troops arrived.

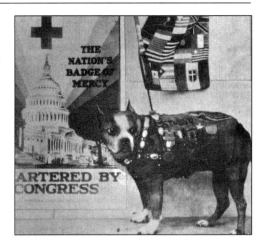

Stubby was the most decorated dog in WWI. Three presidents—Wilson, Harding and Coolidge—invited him to the White House, and he was decorated by General Pershing. Stubby was awarded life memberships in the Red Cross, YMCA and American Legion.

Following the war, the Pit Bull's popularity continued to grow. Depending on what it was used for and where it lived, the breed was still known by many different names, such as Bulldog, American Bull Terrier, Brindle Bull Dog, Yankee Terrier, Pit Dog and, of course, American Pit Bull Terrier. At least one breed club, The American Bull Terrier Club of Clay Center, Kansas, existed as early as 1921. It was headed by F. L. Dunable.

The first Pit Bull movie star was whelped on September 6, 1929. Petey, a brindle and white bred by A. A. Keller, achieved

"Petey" of the Our Gang comedy series, at the Steel Pier in Atlantic City, 1935.

fame on stage and screen as the dog actor in the Little Rascals and the Our Gang comedy series. Owned and trained by Harry Lucenay, Petey's UKC registered name was Lucenay's Peter.

A SEPARATE STRAIN

In May 1936, a group of American Pit Bull Terrier fanciers who wanted to exhibit their dogs at shows formed the Staffordshire Terrier Club of America. The club's purpose was to achieve American Kennel Club (AKC) recognition for the breed, since neither the United Kennel Club nor the American Dog Breeders Association held shows at that time. In June 1936, the breed was accepted by the American Kennel Club under the name Staffordshire Terrier. Some American Pit Bull Terrier breeders immediately switched their dogs over to AKC registration. Others continued to register with UKC and/or ADBA, but registered with the AKC as well. Breeders who had no interest in showing their dogs did not register with AKC.

Not everyone who registered their dogs with AKC during those early years was anti-dogfighting and pro show. Some dogs made a name in both the pit and the ring. For example, Corvino's Braddock, a fourteen-time pit winner, sired AKC Champion Young Joe Braddock, one of the top Staffordshires in

An American Pit Bull Terrier breeder from the 1920s. (Courtesy of Virginia Isaac)

the showring in 1946. But as time passed, fewer and fewer breeders of fighting dogs took part in dog shows and the Staffordshire Terrier (renamed the American Staffordshire Terrier in 1972), became a separate, rather distinct strain within the breed.

During the mid-1970s, both the United Kennel Club and the American Dog Breeders Association began sanctioning shows for American Pit Bull Terriers. Since then, the number of APBTs entered in shows has grown steadily.

MEDIA MONSTER

As the years went by, pockets of underground dogfighting activity continued in the United States. By the late 1960s, some dog lovers were determined to put a stop to it, and by 1970 the American Dog Owner's Association (ADOA) was established for the purpose of terminating dogfighting. The ADOA was instrumental in getting the Animal Welfare Act revised, leading to the arrest of many dogfighters. Meanwhile, the media focused their cameras and commentary on the teeth and muscles of the bloodied, exhausted dogs picked up during police raids on dogfights, instead of on the people who placed those dogs in the pit and wagered on the outcome. A media monster was born, and its name was Pit Bull.

THE MONSTER-MOBSTER CONNECTION

Monsters are exciting. Just look at all the children who dress up like Jason, Freddie, Frankenstein and Dracula on Halloween. It's fun to pretend to be bad for one night. But the headlines and TV stories concocted about the Pit Bull attracted the type of people who weren't pretending. When the media manufactured a "bad dog" monster, young toughs, those who reveled in flaunting their badness, believed that swaggering through their turf with a Pit Bull by their side would enhance their image. When thugs heard theories about teeth that locked and incredible jaw pressure, they not only believed them, but exaggerated them when they bragged. Soon drug dealers, gang members and other hoodlums all wanted a dog like that. Biologists eventually proved these theories ridiculous, but the punks read only headlines, not lengthy, academic reports. So the same breed of dog that laid its life on the line for its dogfighter owners became the preferred mascot of minor mobsters.

It didn't remain the same breed of dog for long. While the dog fighters—and even the bullbaiters before them—never wanted and never bred a dog that was aggressive toward people, the thugs had something else in mind. With no knowledge of genetics or dog breeding, they indiscriminately mated their dogs to larger and nastier dogs of any breed whatsoever. The result was mixed-bred dogs the punks still proudly and defiantly called Pit Bulls. They used them to terrorize their enemies, guard drug caches and slow down the police during drug raids. These dogs, now mixed with Rottweilers, various shepherds and even mean mongrels, are no more American Pit Bull Terriers than puppies from a Border Collie/Labrador Retriever cross are still Border Collies. But the press, and sometimes the courts, still persist in lumping the mobster's mongrels with registered dogs.

Today, the media still love their monster. After all, Pit Bulls sell papers and attract TV viewers. A few years ago there was a *New York Post* story about a man who was attacked and severely bitten on the leg by another breed of dog. He called the local media, but they didn't find it exciting enough to report. So a few days later, out of curiosity, he falsely told the same story to the same media, but this time he said the dog was a Pit Bull. Three television news stations and four newspapers sent reporters immediately.

Also during the late 1980s, in Jacksonville, Florida, an elderly woman stepped outside her home to pick up her newspaper and was attacked and killed by three dogs. The dogs' owner didn't want them put to sleep and thought saying they were purebreds might save them. So he told the police they were English Bull Terriers. But the police wrote English Bulldogs on their report, and the media decided to call them Pit Bulls and give them headlines. Only the animal control people filed it correctly: mixed breeds, possibly with some Boxer.

The result of the rash of Pit Bull headlines across the nation was that some cities sought to pass laws banning the breed. These were challenged by the ADOA, the major dog registries and dog owners in general, as dog clubs dedicated to all breeds soon realized that if one breed was banned, others could easily follow. In most cases, breed-specific wording was revised and the laws that eventually went into effect were vicious dog laws that encompassed all dogs equally. Insurance companies, however, were and still are another problem. Many of them have discriminatory clauses in their policies dealing with several of the stronger breeds, not just the American Pit Bull Terrier.

THE PIT BULL TODAY

The real American Pit Bull Terrier, the one registered with UKC or ADBA, is the same affectionate, reliable, people-loving dog it ever was. And today, because dog shows emphasize balanced structure and fluid movement, and obedience competition emphasizes trainability, the breed is sometimes an even more attractive companion then it used to be.

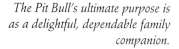
The Pit Bull's ultimate purpose is as a delightful, dependable family companion.

The American Pit Bull Terrier has always been a dog with a strong resolve to please its owner. When that owner wanted his dog to fight, no matter how overmatched the dog was, it fought with gameness. And today, when the Pit Bull's enlightened owner raises his dog to be a happy, dependable family companion, that is exactly what it becomes. No dog does it better.

AGGRESSION

You should never, ever be afraid of your dog. Not for a minute. Not even for an instant. Don't ignore or excuse threatening behavior just because it was over quickly. Next time your dog's threat will be even stronger—and yes, there will be a next time.

If a socialized puppy under six months is seriously threatening family members or friendly strangers by snarling, growling, snapping or biting, it is probably a hopeless case. Aggression toward humans is not natural, and this type of pup was probably born brain damaged or with a genetic fault. For the sake of your family and the rest of the dogs that make up this naturally friendly breed, a people-aggressive puppy should be humanely euthanized. Please don't get rid of a mean puppy by finding it another home. That won't cure its problem and could have tragic consequences for unsuspecting new owners.

A show of aggression sometimes occurs between nine and twelve months old, when the dog reaches sexual maturity and tries to establish its position in the pack (that's the family to you). For example, he may know he isn't the leader because the person called Daddy obviously is, but he may try to dominate the person called Mom. Or perhaps Mom trained him and knows she's dominant, but he's jealous of her attention and growls when Dad or anyone else tries to get close to her. This is the type of aggression that surprises people. The first time their dog growls a challenge at them they quickly explain that he never did that before. But he probably did. They just didn't recognize the signs.

The first sign that a dog is vying for dominance is when he simply ignores a command. You say "Down" and he walks into the other room. He's out of your way, which is what you wanted, so you don't bother to enforce the command and quickly forget the minor disobedience. But your dog doesn't. Another couple of unenforced commands, and he's ready to test you at a higher level. His opportunity comes up a few days later when you are in a hurry to clean up, and you bend to pick up his food dish before he licks the last morsel. He stands over it, body rigid, head cocked and eyes looking straight into yours. "Okay, hurry up and finish it," you say, never realizing that you just lost round two. When round three comes, it may be a growl. Surprised and momentarily fearful, you won't be able to deny that there is a problem, but you'll probably say he never did anything like that before.

This type of escalating aggression is much easier to prevent than it is to correct. First, socialize your puppy well. By meeting many people, your American Pit Bull Terrier learns that almost everyone is a friend. When he needs to differentiate, he will. Don't push it. Never urge your dog to be aggressive toward humans.

Second, teach your dog a few basic commands when he is quite young and use them for everyday life. "Sit" for petting; "Down" for biscuit; "Shake hands" for fun. Never allow your dog to yank you around when you walk him. Perhaps the most important rule for raising a fine dog is, Never give a command you aren't prepared to enforce. For example, don't command your dog to "Come" when you are in the bathtub unless you plan to make wet tracks to him immediately and enforce the command if he ignores you. Dominance is mental and has nothing to do with physical strength or physical punishment. It's as simple as this: When you train your dog and he obeys you, he is content. He knows how to please you, understands that you are dominant and doesn't try to test you.

CHAPTER TWO

The American Pit Bull Terrier, *Now*

PIT BULL PERSONALITY AND HOW IT GOT THAT WAY

The American Pit Bull Terrier, with ancestors created to compete in the most violent blood sports, emerged strong mentally and physically. Its forebears survived by being strong, intelligent and courageous long after survival of the fittest played a role in the propagation of other domestic animals. Partly because of that, the Pit Bull has remained a functional, capable dog. It confidently undertakes the roles of natural guard in the home, competitive weight puller, show dog, agility dog, obedience competitor and children's companion and protector.

When she was good, she was very, very good
But when she was bad, she was horrid.

How did a breed that was especially created to slaughter its own kind become a fine family pet? To find out, we will have to visualize a traditional pit fight. Happily, this cruel sport is illegal today, but in its heyday, the following would have been a typical scenario.

A TRADITIONAL PIT FIGHT

When a dogfighter wanted to match his dog, he decided what would be the best fighting weight for that dog and then opened it up to be matched at that weight. The news was conveyed through the underground world of the dogfighting fraternity, and eventually someone else agreed to match his dog against theirs at that weight. Forfeit money was posted with a trusted third party, and sometimes a written contract was signed.

After the fight was scheduled, the dogs were put into a keep. A keep is a regimen of exercise and diet designed to bring a fighting dog to top strength and endurance without it carrying an extra ounce of weight. During a keep, the handler would use roadwork, a treadmill and possibly a swim tank, rubbing down the dog thoroughly after its exercise sessions. The keep could last anywhere from six weeks to three months, during which time the handler spent several hours a day preparing the dog.

When the handlers and dogs arrived at the fight, a coin was tossed and the winner of the toss chose whether his dog would be washed first or last. Opponents washed each other's dog just before a match. This ensured that neither dog had an evil-tasting substance or even poison on its coat, which would deter or kill the rival dog when it bit.

After each dog was washed and towel-dried, it was wrapped in a towel and carried to its own corner of the pit. The dog knew why it was there. It wouldn't be matched if it hadn't either fought before or been rolled often enough to understand its owner's game. (In dogfighter jargon, a roll is a short practice fight to see if a young dog has pit potential and to give it experience.) Because they knew what was coming next, the dogs were usually agitated by the time they were carried to the pit, and their handlers often tried to calm them in order to conserve their energy.

The match began as soon as the referee gave the release order. When the dogs charged viciously at each other, there were three people in the pit with them: two handlers and the referee. Spectators and bettors around the pit sometimes numbered in the hundreds.

Most Pit Bulls fought silently. Using a combination of power and agility, they wrestled each other in an attempt to gain the advantage of their favorite hold. When reading Pit Bull history books about renowned leg fighters or famous ear fighters, the body part referred to the dog's favorite place to grip its rival. Once a fighting dog clamped down on its opponent, it usually would not release its grip until it saw the opportunity to get a better one, or until the rival dog maneuvered itself free. That's why the majority of dogfight wounds were punctures, not rips and slashes. Matches slowed down considerably when both dogs seemed satisfied with their holds. Sometimes neither one moved for several minutes, except to shake its foe every so often.

During a match, the handlers were often right down on the mat beside their dogs, sometimes whispering to them and sometimes cheering them on. But they weren't allowed to touch their dogs unless ordered to handle by the referee. Sometimes dogs became fanged (caught their own lip with their tooth). When this happened, most referees tried to free the lip themselves, using a pencil to push the lip back up over the tooth. If the referee couldn't loosen the trapped lip, he would order the dogs parted. Then the handlers used breaking sticks (wedge-shaped wooden implements that pried open a dog's mouth) to break the dogs' holds on each other. After the handler of the fanged dog freed its lip, the referee would ask the handlers to face the dogs four feet apart and release them to continue fighting.

When a dog turned its head and shoulders away from its challenger, a turn was called. That meant the handlers had to pick up their dogs and take them back to their respective corners as soon as neither dog had a hold of the other. When each dog was back in its corner, the handler of the dog that turned released his dog. To continue to be a contender, the dog would have to scratch (cross the pit and attack the other dog within ten seconds). From then on, the dogs scratched in turn. When a dog failed to scratch or a handler conceded the match to save his dog's life, the fight ended. A dog that failed to scratch was said to lack gameness and was usually euthanized. A dog that was badly beaten but continued to scratch with gusto was considered game. Such a dog was highly regarded, even if its handler conceded the fight to save its life.

THE CHARACTER OF A PIT DOG

Contrary to popular hysteria and media hype, the dogfighting fraternity neither bred nor trained the Pit Bull to be mean toward people. Imagine anyone wanting to work with a dangerous dog for hours every day in a keep! And how many handlers would agree to a match if they thought they would have to bathe the other handler's vicious man-biter before the fight? Referees would also be in short supply if unfanging strange dogs during the fury of battle resulted in the loss of fingers. In fact, because they were always handled during all sorts of circumstances, fighting dogs had to be friendly, steady and reliable around people. It's part of their history. During the era of bull-baiting, when the bull tossed a dog, its owner tried to break its fall by catching it on his own shoulders. As hurt and angry as the dogs were, they didn't misplace their aggression by biting their owner instead of the bull.

Kelly's Cecil and Alyssa Kelly are best buddies.

Today, a properly bred Pit Bull is so exuberantly happy upon meeting its owner's friends (or even friendly strangers), that new owners sometimes worry that their dog is too sweet and fun-loving to protect their home and family. Never fear. The joyous, turned-on tail thumper that greets a friendly stranger without hesitation is the same dog that will steadfastly stop an unfriendly stranger in his tracks. In fact, one of the attributes of the Pit Bull is its ability to tell the difference. The APBT doesn't need any formal guard training to be a forceful, competent, natural guardian.

The protective instinct of the American Pit Bull Terrier usually surfaces when the dog is approximately ten months old, although this can vary by three months or so in either direction. A Pit Bull with the correct temperament won't threaten to attack a human without a very good reason, but will begin alerting to the doorbell or the sight of a stranger approaching the house. The young dog doesn't need any encouragement to guard its humans and its home, and is best allowed to use its own discretion. There have been numerous cases proving the exceptional ability of the family Pit Bull to sense and communicate to its family when a person or a situation could be

Pit Bulls are natural guardians, on the alert for unfriendly strangers.

dangerous. Exceptions to letting an APBT guard at its own discretion would be if the dog is overly aggressive, or if it is destined to be used in a specific type of protection work.

From their fighting past (and in some unfortunate instances, their fighting present), Pit Bulls developed unique temperament traits. One of these is their ability to be aggressive and affectionate at the same time, and not take out their aggression on a human. Necessary in the pit, this trait allowed handlers to safely pick up their dog during a fight.

In civilized circumstances, the trait sometimes shows up when a Pit Bull is out for a walk on leash and another dog eyes it menacingly. The Pit Bull's immediate reaction might be to face the other dog, ready to take it on. However, if the Pit Bull has had training, and its owner pulls back on the lead, disciplining it for its breech of manners, the dog will often lick its owner in apology. A Pit Bull without sufficient training may go back to threatening the other dog after making up with its owner—in fact, the breed has the ability to display anger in one direction and love in the other direction, back and forth, over and over, without ever misplacing the aggression.

The earliest records of the Bull and Terrier dogs in England show that many of the top fighting dogs had multiple owners. Today, Pit Bulls are known for being highly adaptable. They can change owners and move to another home with ease, provided their new family provides attention and love.

Pit Bulls enjoy being the center of attention, are confident enough to adapt to unusual surroundings and have a high tolerance for pain. Today these traits place them among the top in therapy-dog work. They gleefully show off their obedience training or their favorite tricks at children's hospitals, senior centers and schools for the mentally and physically challenged. Petting sessions often follow the programs, and Pit Bulls excel at giving affection in institutions because they aren't bothered by an occasional bump from a cane or walker. Laying their heads in the laps of the elderly in rockers and children in wheelchairs, they look up lovingly and grunt happily, even when petted or poked a little too hard.

COMICAL COMMUNICATION

One of the reasons American Pit Bull Terriers are so much fun is because their faces are so expressive. Some Pit Bulls actually smile. These special canine clowns greet their owners, and sometimes other human friends, with a large, toothy grin. They make this amusing mug by raising their upper lip until their muzzle wrinkles and their eyes narrow. When smiling, many Pit Bulls also tap their front feet up and down in a happy dance, demonstrating their delight at the sight of a loved one. While this facial expression is comical and endearing to those who know the breed, it has been known to terrify friendly strangers.

Some breeds of dogs are uncomfortable about meeting a human's look head on, but not the APBT. Not only do they seem to enjoy looking directly into a person's eyes, but they have a charming way of wrinkling their foreheads and cocking their heads, demonstrating that they are giving you their absolute attention.

When a Pit Bull believes it has been treated unfairly or slighted, it may turn its back on its owner and refuse to look directly at him. This behavior appears to be the dog's way of

Pit Bulls can be real clowns. Here Spartan's Samson sticks his tongue out while posing with Santa.

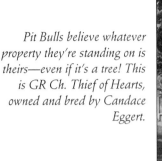

Pit Bulls believe whatever property they're standing on is theirs—even if it's a tree! This is GR Ch. Thief of Hearts, owned and bred by Candace Eggert.

declaring, "We're not on speaking terms right now." But Pit Bulls are too devoted and fun-loving to hold a grudge for long, so if your dog tries to take you on a guilt trip, let it pout in peace and it will soon be back at your side.

COMMON CHARACTERISTICS

The Pit Bull was bred for generations with the emphasis on mental attitude and character. In this breed, appearance is a relatively recent concern, and a Pit Bull that lacks true breed character is considered a pathetic caricature no matter how handsome he is. Personalities differ in individual dogs, but certain characteristics should be inherent in every member of this breed.

The typical Pit Bull exudes self-confidence, not only at home, but in the park or on a noisy city street. It doesn't respect territorial rights as so many other breeds of dogs do, but acts like whatever property it happens to be standing on is his. While degree of aggression toward other dogs varies with individuals, a Pit Bull may be so self-assured that it ignores other breeds rather than picking fights to prove itself. However, this is not always the case. Owners should be aware that from nine months of age on, their Pit Bull could suddenly develop a desire to test its strength against other dogs. That's one of the reasons training is so important. When a Pit Bull is socialized and trained (see Chapter 7), its owner has the tools to end aggressive behavior toward other dogs before it becomes a problem.

The APBT is outgoing with people, sometimes even overly friendly, provided its owner is present and obviously trusts the person. It has a joyful disposition, loves to play and is somewhat of a perennial puppy as it enjoys games of tug, catch and sometimes fetch, well into old age. Some Pit Bulls race through the house now and then as a comical outlet for their high spirits. A few Pit Bulls are escape artists, able to jump or climb six-foot or higher fences. Others have taught themselves to open gates.

Some Pit Bulls of either sex are maternal with baby animals of almost any species, and females have been known to wet-nurse almost anything, from orphaned kittens to potbellied pigs. Although most Pit Bulls dislike strange cats, they will live peacefully with the family cat.

Robust and brimming with vigor, the Pit Bull is an intelligent roughneck that wants to please. It is good-natured with children, has the sturdiness not to mind if its tail or toe is accidentally stepped on and possesses the capacity to play for hours. Many Pit Bulls seem to sense which children enjoy rough-and-tumble games and which ones are too tiny for such shenanigans.

HANDLING TIPS

When bringing home a new baby, give your Pit Bull attention as before and talk to it while you care for the baby. If you don't shove your dog aside as if it were suddenly an unloved nuisance, it will quickly realize that the new baby is under its protection, the same as the rest of the family.

Many Pit Bulls have a stubborn streak when it comes to training and may become pouty when pushed to learn something they don't care to do. The trick is to remain persistent and firm with no loss of temper. Pit Bulls simply need to believe that their owner is even more stubborn than they are. When your dog fully understands what you want it to do and realizes you're not going to quit, it will master the exercise. APBTs accept fair corrections with good spirit, have incredibly good memories and love praise. Once they learn something, they soon perform as if it were their idea all along.

DEFECTIVE DOGS

American Pit Bull Terriers with temperament problems are rare exceptions, but these exceptions must be mentioned because a dangerous disposition is a menace to your family, your neighbors and the breed itself. Every breed produces occasional problem dogs, which never become enjoyable companions, but the Pit Bull is simply too strong and capable to be allowed mental instability. Beware of the extremes—dogs that are either aggressive or extremely timid around people. People-aggressive Pit Bulls are not representative of the breed and are far too dangerous to be pets. Painfully shy dogs are also atypical, and may grow into fear-biters.

Responsible breeders are careful to choose animals of fine character for breeding stock, but an infrequent bad dog still may be born. Even with the best breeding pair, rare problems such as too little oxygen during birth or a tumor on the brain can destroy what would have been a delightful disposition.

While bad temperaments due to heredity are rare in registered American Pit Bull Terriers, some dogs become unstable because of their environment. Here are the three most common reasons why a perfectly nice puppy might grow up mentally defective:

1. Certain types of people delight in owning a dangerous dog. Such a person might acquire a friendly puppy and encourage it to become mean. Eager to please, the dog will grow up to be just as bad as its owner desires.
2. Unfair and overly harsh discipline can reduce an outgoing pup to a cowering bundle of nerves—the first step on the way to fear-biting. Patience, persistence and praise

are essential when working with puppies, and no one should ever train a dog of any age when he or she is in a bad mood.

3. Neglect probably negates more happy-go-lucky puppy personalities than any other sin of dog ownership. Seldom done on purpose, it just seems to happen when the newness of having a puppy wears off. Soon the youngster is constantly confined to a crate, tie-out chain, kennel or yard with no human contact except at feeding time. Lonely, bored and isolated from its human family, the puppy will be unable to develop its unique character, and could become aloof, shy or cranky.

REALITY, PLEASE

These are the years of the Pit Bull horror stories. Other breeds suffered and survived when the stigma was on them, and since no breed is a better survivor than the American Pit Bull Terrier, it will still be our companion when it becomes fashionable to blame every bite on some other breed. But don't be surprised by the crazy comments you may elicit when you walk your cute puppy down the street. Here's a sample of what you might hear:

1. "Aren't you afraid it will bite your children?"
2. "Is it true that dogfighters train them by having them kill baby kittens?"
3. "Isn't that one of those dogs that can lock its jaws shut?"
4. "Susie, stay away from that dog!"
5. "Wow, a Pit Bull. Those dogs can bite harder than any other dog."
6. "What an adorable puppy. May I pet it?"

You'll hear No. 6 the most often, and the answer to it is, Yes. Meeting nice people will help your puppy develop its personality to its fullest potential.

The answer to Nos. 1 through 5 is to smile and keep walking. If you try to defend your dog to everyone who voices a preconceived opinion, you won't have any fun on your walks. For your information:

1. The original Bull and Terrier dog was nicknamed "The Children's Nursemaid" in England.
2. No, it isn't true. Killing baby kittens would do nothing at all to condition a fighting dog.
3. Biologists studying the skulls, mandibles and teeth of Pit Bulls have found no evidence of a locking mechanism. In fact, they've found nothing at all unique about the jaws or teeth of the APBT. They are similar to those of every other breed of dog.
4. Poor Susie. Maybe her momma will let her pet some other dog.
5. Biologists say that data describing the biting power of dogs in pounds per square inch have not been collected because there is no meaningful way to gather such information. Figures relating to the biting power of Pit Bulls have been published in newspaper articles, but it is simply rumor with no scientific foundation.

If your close friends are worried about your choice of a dog, tell them you are in good company. Other Pit Bull owners have included Thomas Edison, inventor; Sir Walter Scott, author; Theodore Roosevelt, U.S. president; Fred Astaire, actor; James Caan, actor; Jack Dempsey, heavyweight champion; Helen Keller, handicapped author and teacher; Michael J. Fox, actor; and Jan Michael Vincent, actor.

ATTRACTIVE OPPOSITES

Strong and sensitive; rowdy yet gentle; outgoing but devoted; easily fired up but highly trainable; mischievous yet sensible; energetic and serene; peaceful, but ever alert—these apparent contradictions could all describe the same American Pit Bull Terrier. The APBT's zest for life, combined with its occasional attempts to outwit its owner, endear the breed to many but

The APBT's zest for life endears it to many. Fonseca's HK Spot decides driving would be more fun than pulling this cart.

could be considered an inconvenience by others. Some people enjoy a little less dog.

Always ready for a romp, the Pit Bull is content to curl up and watch television when playtime ends. He does his relaxing from three favorite positions. One is a head-in-the-lapside seat, the other is frog position on the rug and the funniest is flat on his back on an easy chair with his head loosely dangling over the edge. But no matter how accomplished a Pit Bull becomes at unwinding, a strange noise brings him to immediate attention, ready and extremely able to defend his family.

WHY STARFIRE SHINES

An example of the ultimate versatile Pit Bull, National Gr. Ch., U-CD, Gr. Ch. Chandy's Lil Starfire, CGC, OFA, began life as the last pick in a litter of puppies bred by Brian Williams in 1989. She was purchased by Candace and Duane Eggert of Long Beach, California. They took her to obedience school and she earned her U-CD with high scores.

Following their success at obedience trials, the Eggerts tried Starfire in conformation competition. Not only did she become a Grand Champion, but 1992 she won the prestigious National Championship .

Yet when the Eggert's talk about their beloved Starfire, they concentrate on other incidents—those that occur outside of competition.

National Ch. U-CD, Gr. Ch. Candy's Lil Starfire, CCC, OFA, with owner-handler Candace Eggert after a 1992 win.

Every year Starfire represents her breed at the Pomona Pet Fair, where thousands of visitors remember the impression left by the friendly, reliable American Pit Bull Terrier. In addition, Starfire frequently visits the local orphanage where the children enjoy her company while learning about canine behavior and service dogs. But cheery Starfire has a serious side, too. One day Duane left her in the van while he ran a quick errand. As he returned and got into the van, Starfire flew across the seats with her teeth bared. Duane looked to the left in time to see a man with his hand on the door change direction so quickly that he nearly fell over his own feet. The man had followed Duane without his realizing it, and Starfire's alert response averted a potentially dangerous situation.

Starfire with people at a pet fair.

Starfire's daughter, Nikki, required a cesarian section with her first litter of puppies. The operation sometimes inhibits the maternal instinct, and when Nikki came out of surgery she showed no interest in caring for her pups. Starfire was obviously concerned about the newborns, so the Eggerts allowed her in the whelping box. She quickly cleaned every puppy, gathered up the litter in the crook of her belly and kept them warm while they tried to suckle. She actually had milk by the next morning, and was able to feed them. Nikki watched Starfire care for the puppies, and eventually her own maternal instinct emerged and she took over. Starfire bowed out graciously, but always enjoyed playing with that litter.

Starfire with grandpuppies she helped raise.

CHAPTER THREE

Who's Who in the Bull and Terrier Breeds

The American Pit Bull Terrier may have been known by more names throughout its history than any other breed of dog. From the time the original Bulldogs were bred to the various game terriers of the British Isles, and through its years of development in the United States, the breed was known as Bull and Terrier; Half-and-Half; Bulldog; Brindle Bull Dog; Pit Dog; Pit Bull; Yankee Terrier; American Bull Terrier; Pit Bull Terrier; and American (Pit) Bull Terrier. During some periods, the breed was known by several of those names at once, depending upon its location and use.

Today, the dogs most often confused with the American Pit Bull Terrier belong to one of three terrier breeds that also evolved from the original Bulldog and terrier crosses. They are the Staffordshire Bull Terrier, the Bull Terrier and the American Staffordshire Terrier. The following descriptions focus on how to differentiate each breed from the American Pit Bull Terrier, and include each breed's standard.

Every breed has a standard. Written by the national (parent) club that represents the breed, the standard is like a blueprint in words, describing the appearance of the ideal or perfect specimen of that breed. Reputable breeders think of the standard as an explanation of excellence, and strive to produce animals that come as close to it as possible. It is also used by dog show judges. Their responsibility is to select as winners those dogs that appear to be the most like their breed's standards. Because the standard provides such a thorough description of a breed, it is useful when comparing similar breeds as an aid to discovering their subtle differences. The following are comparative descriptions and the breed standards of the Staffordshire Bull Terrier, the Bull Terrier, the American Staffordshire Terrier and the American Pit Bull Terrier.

THE STAFFORDSHIRE BULL TERRIER

With a height of between fourteen and sixteen inches at the withers (the highest point of the shoulder blades, found just behind the base of the neck), and a weight of between twenty-four and thirty-eight pounds, the Staffordshire Bull Terrier is the modern breed most similar in appearance to the original Bull and Terrier dogs of the British Isles. Because dogfighting was its original purpose, the breed was not recognized by the Kennel Club of England, its country of origin, until 1935. By then it had proved its worth many times over as a playful pet and devoted guardian. In the United States, the breed is registered by the American Kennel Club (AKC) and the United Kennel Club (UKC).

The most obvious difference between the Staffordshire Bull Terrier and the American Pit Bull Terrier is size. While sturdy and strong, the Stafford is a smaller dog all around, being shorter in height and anywhere from ten to thirty pounds lighter than the Pit Bull. At a dog show, the Staffordshire Bull Terrier is always exhibited with natural ears (uncropped), and nearly all pet Staffords are also uncropped. While both the Stafford and

A Staffordshire Bull Terrier. This is Little Nell, owned by Marion Lane.

the Pit Bull have straight forelegs, the Stafford's feet should turn outward slightly.

The following is the breed standard for the Staffordshire Bull Terrier, as approved by the American Kennel Club in November 1989.

General Appearance—The Staffordshire Bull Terrier is a smooth-coated dog. It should be of great strength for its size and, although muscular, should be active and agile.

Size, Proportion, Substance—Height at shoulder: fourteen to sixteen inches. Weight: Dogs, twenty-eight to thirty-eight pounds; bitches, twenty-four to thirty-four pounds, these heights being related to weights. Nonconformity with these limits is a fault. In proportion, the length of back, from withers to tailset, is equal to the distance from withers to ground.

Head—Short, deep through, broad skull, very pronounced cheek muscles, distinct stop, short foreface, black nose. Pink (Dudley) nose to be considered a serious fault. **Eyes**—Dark preferable, but may bear some relation to coat color. Round, of medium size, and set to look straight ahead. Light eyes or pink eye rims to be considered a fault, except that where the coat surrounding the eye is white the eye rim may be pink. **Ears**—Rose or half-pricked and not large. Full drop or full prick to be considered a serious fault. **Mouth**—A bite in which the outer side of the lower incisors touches the inner side of the upper incisors. The lips should be tight and clean. The badly undershot or overshot bite is a serious fault.

Neck, Topline, Body—The neck is muscular, rather short, clean in outline and gradually widening toward the shoulders. The body is close coupled, with a level topline, wide front, deep brisket and well-sprung ribs being rather light in the loins. The tail is undocked, of medium length, low set, tapering to a point and carried rather low. It should not curl much and may be likened to an old-fashioned pump handle. A tail that is too long or badly curled is a fault.

Forequarters—Legs straight and well boned, set rather far apart, without looseness at the shoulders and showing no weakness at the pasterns, from which point the feet turn out a little. Dewclaws on the forelegs may be removed. The feet should be well padded, strong and of medium size.

Hindquarters—The hindquarters should be well muscled, hocks let down with stifles well bent. Legs should be parallel when viewed from behind. Dewclaws, if any, on the hind legs are generally removed. Feet as in front.

Coat—Smooth, short and close to the skin, not to be trimmed or dewhiskered.

Color—Red, fawn, white, black or blue, or any of these colors with white. Any shade of brindle or any shade of brindle with white. Black and tan or liver color to be disqualified.

Gait—Free, powerful and agile with economy of effort. Legs moving parallel when viewed from front or rear. Discernible drive from hind legs.

Temperament—From the past history of the Staffordshire Bull Terrier, the modern dog draws its character of indomitable courage, high intelligence and tenacity. This, coupled with its affection for its friends, and children in particular, its off-duty quietness and trustworthy stability, makes it a foremost all-purpose dog.

Disqualification—Black and tan or liver color.

For additional information on the Staffordshire Bull Terrier, contact the Staffordshire Bull Terrier Club, Inc., 24451 Dartmouth, Dearborn Heights, MI 48125.

THE BULL TERRIER

In the 1850s, James Hinks, a dog breeder from Birmingham, England, began the experimentation that led to the origin of the Bull Terrier. Starting with the most rugged and tenacious Bull and Terrier dogs, he added some White English Terrier (now extinct) and a touch of Dalmatian and Spanish Pointer in an effort to create an all-white dog that would be the fiercest of all canine gladiators.

His newly developed breed was both a failure and a popularly acclaimed success. Although courageous and energetic, the dog Hinks called the Bull Terrier would just as soon frolic as fight. Hinks's son wrote of his father's dogs, "...in short, they became the old fighting dog civilized, with all his rough edges smoothed down without being softened; alert, active, plucky, muscular and a real gentleman. Naturally, this change brought the Bull Terrier many admirers, and the milk-white dog became the fashion."

Hinks exhibited his new breed at a dog show in 1862, and the dogs gained a following so quickly that by 1888 there was a Bull Terrier club in England. The Bull Terrier Club of America,

White Bull Terrior Ch. Radar of Monty-Ayr.

established in 1895, is one of the oldest terrier clubs in the United States.

The Bull Terrier's head immediately identifies the breed. At first sight some find it beautiful and others find it ugly, but all realize that it is unique. Seen from the front, the Bull Terrier's face is oval, and its breed standard describes it as "egg shaped." The head should be filled up completely, like a blown-up balloon, so the surface has no humps, hollows or indentations.

From the side, the face is equally distinctive. Termed down-faced or Roman-nosed, there is no stop (indentation) where the muzzle meets the skull, and even the tip of the nose bends downward in the best specimens. The Bull Terrier has naturally pricked ears that are never cropped. Its unusual eyes are small, sunk into the head, obliquely placed, triangular in shape and very dark, piercing and expressive.

The Bull Terrier comes in two varieties, white and colored. The Colored Bull Terrier was developed by crossing the White Bull Terrier with the Staffordshire Bull Terrier. Recognized as a variety in 1936, it differs from the white only in color.

The following is the breed standard for the Bull Terrier, as approved by the American Kennel Club in July 1974.

White Bull Terrier

The white Bull Terrier must be strongly built, muscular, symmetrical and active, with a keen, determined and intelligent expression, full of fire but of sweet disposition and amenable to discipline.

Head—Should be long, strong and deep right to the end of the muzzle, but not coarse. Full face it should be oval in outline and be filled up completely, giving the impression of fullness with a surface devoid of hollows or indentations; i.e., egg shaped. In profile it should curve gently downwards from the top of the skull to the tip of the nose. The forehead should be flat across from ear to ear. The distance from the tip of the nose to the eyes should be perceptibly greater than that from the eyes to the top of the skull. The underjaw should be deep and well defined. **Lips**—Clean and tight. **Teeth**—Meet in either a level or a scissors bite. In the scissors bite the upper teeth should fit in front of and closely against the lower teeth, and they should be sound, strong and perfectly regular. **Ears**—Small, thin and placed close together. They should be capable of being held stiffly erect, when they should point upwards. **Eyes**—Well sunken and as dark as possible, with a piercing glint, and they should be small, triangular and obliquely placed; set near together and high up on the dog's head. Blue eyes are a disqualification. **Nose**—Black, with well-developed nostrils bent downward at the tip.

Neck—Should be very muscular, long, arched and clean, tapering from the shoulders to the head and it should be free from loose skin. The chest should be broad when viewed from in front, and there should be great depth from withers to brisket, so that the latter is nearer the ground than the belly.

Body—Should be well rounded with marked spring of rib, the back should be short and strong. The back ribs deep. Slightly arched over the loin. The shoulders should be strong and muscular but without heaviness. The shoulder blades should be wide and flat and there should be a very pronounced backward slope from the bottom edge of the blade to the top edge. Behind the shoulders there should be no slackness or dip at the withers. The underline from the brisket to the belly should form a graceful upward curve.

Legs—Should be big boned but not to the point of coarseness; the forelegs should be of moderate length, perfectly straight, and the dog must stand firmly upon them. The elbows must turn neither in nor out, and the pasterns should be strong and upright. The hind legs should be parallel viewed from behind. The thighs very muscular with hocks well let down. Hind pasterns short and upright. The stifle joint should be well bent with a well-developed second thigh. The feet should be round and compact with well-arched toes like a cat.

Tail—Should be short, set on low, fine and ideally should be carried horizontally. It should be thick where it joins the body, and should taper to a fine point.

Coat—Should be short, flat, harsh to the touch and with a fine gloss. The dog's skin should fit tightly. The color is white, though markings on the head are permissible. Any markings elsewhere on the coat are to be severely faulted. Skin pigmentation is not to be penalized.

Movement—The dog shall move smoothly, covering the ground with free, easy strides, fore and hind legs should move parallel each to each when viewed from in front or behind. The forelegs reaching out well and hind legs moving smoothly at the hip and flexing well at the stifle and hock. The dog should move compactly and in one piece but with a typical jaunty air that suggests agility and power.

Faults—Any departure from the foregoing points shall be considered a fault, and the seriousness of the fault shall be in exact proportion to its degree; i.e., a very crooked front is a very bad fault; a rather crooked front is a rather bad fault; and a slightly crooked front is a slight fault.

Disqualification—Blue eyes.

Colored Bull Terrier

The standard for the colored Bull Terrier is the same as for the white except for the subhead "Color," which reads:

Color—Any color other than white, or any color with white markings. Other things being equal, the preferred color is brindle. A dog that is predominantly white shall be disqualified.

Disqualifications—Blue eyes. Any dog that is predominantly white.

For additional information on the colored or white Bull Terrier, contact the Bull Terrier Club of America, 10477 Ethel Cr., Cypress, CA 90630.

THE MINIATURE BULL TERRIER

The Miniature Bull Terrier is a sturdy, courageous, smaller version of the Bull Terrier. Weighing around sixteen pounds, the Mini Bull is identical to the full-sized Bull Terrier in shape and temperament. Consequently, both its size and its head shape easily differentiate it from the American Pit Bull Terrier.

For additional information on Miniature Bull Terriers, contact the Miniature Bull Terrier Club, Education Coordinator, 16 Fremont Road, Sandown, NH 03873.

THE AMERICAN STAFFORDSHIRE TERRIER AND THE AMERICAN PIT BULL TERRIER

The American Staffordshire Terrier is the dog most easily confused with the American Pit Bull Terrier—and for good reason. The Bull and Terrier dog that was developed in the British Isles evolved into the modern Staffordshire Bull Terrier. But when the Bull and Terrier dog arrived in America, it was selectively bred to be taller and heavier. In fact, it was changed enough to be considered a separate breed. That breed was the American Pit Bull Terrier. So where did the American Staffordshire Terrier come from?

The American Staffordshire Terrier (known as the Staffordshire Terrier from 1936 until 1972) is the American Kennel Club–registered version of the American Pit Bull Terrier. Although the United Kennel Club began registering American Pit Bull Terriers in 1898 and the American Dog Breeders Association opened its registry in 1909, neither of them held dog shows. The AKC did sanction shows, so in the early 1930s, a group of Pit Bull owners who wanted to show their dogs formed a club for the purpose of obtaining AKC recognition for the breed. They succeeded, and the breed was granted AKC recognition in 1936 under the name Staffordshire Terrier. The name change was requested by the AKC because that organization felt that the word "Pit" in the breed's popular name carried an innuendo of dogfighting.

Does that mean Pit Bulls and American Staffordshire Terriers are exactly the same and only the name is different? Well, yes and no. When the breed was granted AKC recognition, there wasn't any great rush to register. Some people detested the

Ch. Kirkee's Polar Bear O'Fraja, CD, an American Staffordshire Terrier National Specialty winner co-owned, bred and handled by Jacqueline O'Neil.

name Staffordshire Terrier, and only those who wanted to show were eager to register with AKC. The first month after recognition was granted, only a dozen dogs were AKC-registered. The second month brought seventeen more, the third month a dozen more and another eleven were registered the fourth month. Registrations continued to trickle in as more and more people became involved in the sport of showing dogs. Eventually AKC closed its Stud Book to the American Pit Bull Terrier and recognized litters only from sires and dams that were already AKC-registered as Staffordshire Terriers. Breeders who had registered their dogs with the AKC mated them with other AKC dogs so the puppies could also be registered and shown. Carefully bred as close as possible to its standard, groomed, taught social graces and shown in the breed and obedience rings, the American Staffordshire was sometimes jokingly referred to as "a Pit Bull wearing a tuxedo."

The practice of breeding AKC Staffordshires to other AKC Staffordshires has continued for about sixty years now. Sixty years is a long time when selectively breeding dogs—so long, in fact, that the AKC version is now a kind of strain within a breed.

So Pit Bulls and American Staffordshire Terriers are not the same because sixty years of selective breeding produced some changes. The average American Staffordshire Terrier is more standardized in size than the average Pit Bull. It is seldom seen in all white, liver or black and tan, as these colors are not considered desirable in that breed. According to the breed standard, American Staffordshire Terrier noses should be solid black, and their eyes are supposed to be dark, while American Pit Bull Terrier eyes and noses may come in any color.

Even so, neither the American Staffordshire Terrier nor the Pit Bull has become standardized to the extreme. Some dogs of either breed still lean toward the original Bulldog in appearance, being shorter of leg and broader of body with larger heads and bulkier muscles. Others are more terrier-like and stand taller, with smoother muscles, a quicker gait and a more refined head.

When are Pit Bulls and American Staffordshire Terriers exactly the same? They are the same when the same dog is registered with both the AKC and the UKC. When the AKC accepted the breed, some APBT owners registered their dogs as Staffordshires with the AKC, while maintaining their American Pit Bull Terrier registrations; they continued to register their dogs with two or more organizations for many years. Those who bought puppies from these breeders received both AKC and UKC papers (the vast majority of dual-registered dogs were in those two organizations), and many people still register their dogs with both organizations today. So quite a few dogs are dual-registered as both UKC American Pit Bull Terriers and AKC American Staffordshire Terriers.

Also, during the mid-1970s, both the UKC and the ADBA began holding dog shows. Breeders who became involved in showing at that time have been selectively breeding for fine conformation for nearly twenty years now. Consequently, it has become extremely difficult, if not impossible, to tell a top show specimen American Pit Bull Terrier from a top show specimen American Staffordshire Terrier.

The American Kennel Club (AKC) standard for the American Staffordshire Terrier and both the United Kennel Club (UKC) and the American Dog Breeders Association (ADBA) standards

A dual champion: UKC and ADBA Ch. Hurricane Hel's Belle with owner-handlers Cheryl and Jeff Helton.

of the American Pit Bull Terrier follow for comparison. Although the American Pit Bull Terrier standards are more lenient on coat, eye and nose color, the standards have more similarities than differences.

The following is the breed standard for the **American Staffordshire Terrier,** as approved by the AKC in June 1936.

General Appearance—The American Staffordshire Terrier should give the impression of great strength for its size, a well-put-together dog, muscular, but agile and graceful, keenly alive to its surroundings. It should be stocky, not long-legged or racy in outline. Its courage is proverbial.

Head—Medium length, deep through, broad skull, very pronounced cheek muscle, distinct stop; ears are set high. **Ears**—Cropped or uncropped, the latter preferred. Uncropped ears should be short and held half rose or prick. Full drop to be penalized. [*Author's note: This is a mistake in the wording of the standard. It should read: uncropped ears should be rose or half prick.*] **Eyes**—Dark and round, low down in skull and set far apart. No pink eyelids. **Muzzle**—Medium length, rounded on upper side to fall away abruptly below eyes. Jaws well defined. Underjaw to be strong and have biting power. Lips close and even, no looseness. Upper teeth to meet tightly outside lower teeth in front. Nose definitely black.

Neck—Heavy, slightly arched, tapering from shoulders to back of skull. No looseness of skin. Medium length.

Shoulders—Strong and muscular with blades wide and sloping.

Back—Fairly short. Slight sloping from withers to rump with gentle short slope at rump to base of tail. Loins slightly tucked.

Body—Well-sprung ribs, deep in rear. All ribs close together. Forelegs set rather wide apart to permit chest development. Chest deep and broad.

Tail—Short in comparison to size, low set, tapering to a fine point; not curled or held over back. Not docked.

Legs—The front legs should be straight, large or round bones, pastern upright. No resemblance of bend in front. Hindquarters well muscled, let down at hocks, turning neither in nor out. Feet of moderate size, well arched and compact. Gait must be springy but without roll or pace.

Coat—Short, close, stiff to the touch and glossy.

Color—Any color, solid, parti, or patched is permissible, but all white, more than 80 percent white, black and tan, and liver not to be encouraged.

Size—Height and weight should be in proportion. A height of about eighteen to nineteen inches at the shoulders for the male and seventeen to eighteen inches for the female is to be considered preferable.

Faults—Faults to be penalized are: Dudley nose, light or pink eyes, tail too long or badly carried, undershot or overshot mouths.

For additional information on the American Staffordshire Terrier, contact the Staffordshire Terrier Club of America, 785 Valley View Road, Forney, TX 75126.

AMERICAN PIT BULL TERRIER STANDARD OF THE UNITED KENNEL CLUB

The following is the breed standard for the American Pit Bull Terrier as approved by the United Kennel Club (UKC) in January 1978.

Head—Medium length. Bricklike in shape. Skull flat and widest at the ears, with prominent cheeks free from wrinkles.

Muzzle—Square, wide and deep. Well-pronounced jaws, displaying strength. Upper teeth should meet tightly over lower teeth, outside in front.

Ears—Cropped or uncropped (not important). Should set high on head, and be free from wrinkles.

Eyes—Round. Should set far apart, low down on skull. Any color acceptable.

Nose—Wide open nostrils. Any color acceptable.

Neck—Muscular. Slightly arched. Tapering from shoulder to head. Free from looseness of skin.

Shoulders—Strong and muscular, with wide sloping shoulder blades.

Back—Short and strong. Slightly sloping from withers to rump. Slightly arched at loins, which should be slightly tucked.

Chest—Deep, but not too broad, with wide sprung ribs.

Ribs—Close. Well-sprung, with deep back ribs.

Tail—Short in comparison to size. Set low and tapering to a fine point. Not carried over back. Bobbed tail not acceptable.

Legs—Large, round boned, with straight, upright pasterns, reasonably strong. Feet to be of medium size. Gait should be light and springy. No rolling or pacing.

Thigh—Long with muscles developed. Hocks down and straight.

Coat—Glossy. Short and stiff to the touch.

Color—Any color or marking permissible.

Weight—Not important. Females preferred from thirty to fifty pounds. Males from thirty-five to sixty pounds.

AMERICAN PIT BULL TERRIER BASIS OF CONFORMATION OF THE AMERICAN DOG BREEDERS ASSOCIATION

The American Dog Breeders Association presents its conformation standard in a different format, as follows:

Experience with dogs, horses, human athletes, cattle, hogs and chickens indicates that for everything that lives and breathes there is an army of experts to tell you how that particular thing should *look*.

Head study of Fonseca's H.K. Shamus, a Therapy Dog owned by Virginia Isaac.

A lot of these experts seem to lack the ability to quantitatively distinguish one physical attribute from another. Most start with an animal they love and build a standard to fit, but some few are really awesome in their knowledge of which physical dimensions work best.

Those persons whose opinions on conformation have borne the test of years have without exception, come from the ranks of the professionals who use the animals to make money. There are cattlemen who can look at two hundred calves and pick the ten best gainers by looking at their conformation. A year later those same calves bring more profit than their less well conformed brothers. Race horse men are the most knowledgeable conformation people you will meet. They all like the same basic things in a horse; although they claim to differ greatly, their differences are minute. As evidence, look at the bidding at a yearling sale when a foal of good conformation is brought in and compare it with the prices offered for an equally well bred foal with conformation faults. Good cattlemen and good horsemen judge conformation by what the animal is supposed to *do*. Cattlemen know from experience that they will lose money feeding narrow shouldered, hollow backed, long-legged calves. Horsemen know that shallow girthed, crooked legged horses with straight hocks seldom cross the finish line first, and that's where the money is.

Now, money doesn't give you good judgment, but it takes good judgment to hang on to it. You can bet that anyone dealing with cattle, horses or Pit Bulls for a long period of time professionally has been exercising good judgment.

Professionals look for an animal that can get the job done. Amateurs, because they have no way to test their theories, wind up feeding their imaginations.

So let's get to the point of establishing a conformation standard for the American Pit Bull Terrier. If we are going to be forced by the laws and today's social standards into breeding a dog for looks rather than performance, in the interest of preserving the most extraordinary animal that man has ever created, let's take a good look at what the American Pit Bull Terrier was supposed to *do*.

His existence today was not because he was bred *only* for gameness. He was not bred *only* for power. He sure as hell was not bred only for his intelligence, loyalty, boldness, round eye, rose ear, red nose or his inclination for dragging children from the paths of speeding trains. He was bred to *win*. That's right folks, he was developed for sporting competition.

The professional dog fighters have made him what he is. The professional dog fighters improved him, and now, when the professional dog fighters are gone, the real Pit Bull Terrier will gradually fade away. What we will have is something the amateurs will have preserved that *reminds* us of the gladiators of old.

Thank God for the amateurs; professional dog fighting is a fast dying occupation. Preservation of this grand athlete that was bred to go to war is going to be in the hands of the amateurs. So, let's look to the profession of the dog in establishing our standard, so that our grandchildren will at least see an authentic physical reproduction of a fighting dog.

If we start with the premise that conformation should reflect the ideal for the dogs usage and that this particular animal was supposed to win a dogfight, we come naturally to the question, what did it take to win?

The APBT was bred for many qualities, and it's up to breeders to preserve them. Here Jessica Gibson shows off Wilder Red Inferno from her father's Southern Pride Kennels.

Most of those who have backed their judgment with hard-earned money would agree on the following to some degree or another.

1. Gameness
2. Attitude
3. Stamina
4. Wrestling ability
5. Biting ability

Note that only one of these qualities, wrestling ability, is directly related to conformation. One other, stamina, may be partly due to conformation, but is probably as much reliant on inherited efficiency of the heart and circulatory system. Some people seem to feel that the shape of the head determines hard bite, but in practice, it seems there are a lot of other factors involved. Earl Tudor said that the great "Black Jack," who killed 4 opponents in 7 big wins in big money fights, bit hard "because he wanted to bite hard." That about sums it up. Good biters seem to be where you find them regardless of the shapes of their heads.

When we talk of conformation we really only mean one thing—wrestling ability. This is the reason the American Pit Bull Terrier varies so much in conformation. His wrestling by itself was not nearly as important as the sum total of gameness, attitude, bite and natural stamina, none of which are directly related to conformation.

Any old time dog fighter would have told you, "If you've got a game dog with good air, he's worth a bet." I might add, "If he can also bite, put a second mortgage on the house and take him to a convention." In other words, never mind what he looks like.

However, wiser men than I have said, "The only dead game dogs are dead ones." Also, "Under certain conditions most dogs will quit." I believe there's a lot of truth to that, and to reinforce the fact that conformation is important, remember that conformation and wrestling ability are very closely related and it's usually the bottom dog in the fight that quits. It's hard to stop even the rankest cur if he can stay on top. The dog whose muscle and bone structure doesn't permit him to wrestle on even terms, needs more of everything else to win. He's always coming from behind. His career is short because each "go" takes so much out of him. So I believe that wrestling ability (and therefore conformation) is a very important ingredient in a fighting dog.

Our standard of Conformation cannot be based on what someone who never saw a dogfight *thinks* a fighting dog should look like, but should be based on those physical attributes displayed by *winning pit dogs*.

American PBT Conformation

Look first at the overall profile of the dog. Ideally, he should be "square" when viewed from the side. That is, about as long from the shoulder to the point of his hip as he is tall from the top of the shoulder to the ground. Such a dog will stand high and have maximum leverage for his weight. This means that standing normally with the hock slightly back of the hip, the dog's base (where his feet are) will be slightly longer than his height. Using the hip and shoulder as guides will keep the viewer from being fooled by the way the dog is standing.

Height to weight ratio is critical. Since dogs were fought at nearly identical weights, the bigger the dog you have at the weight, the better your chances. Hence, stocky dogs with long bodies, heavy shoulders and thick legs usually lose to taller, rangier opponents.

In APBTs, height-to-weight ratio is critical. This is Cheryl Helton's Ch. 'PR' Dogwoods Diablo.

Nature usually blesses a tall rangy dog with a fairly long neck, which is a tremendous advantage in that it enables him to reach a stifle when his opponent may have his front leg, take an ear to hold off a shorter necked opponent, or to reach the chest himself when the other dog is trying to hold him off. The neck should be heavily muscled right up to the base of the skull.

Secondly, look at his back end. That's the drive train of any four legged animal. A Bulldog does 80 percent of his work off his hips and back legs.

A long sloping hip is most important. By its very length, it gives leverage to the femur or thigh bone. A long hip will give the dog a slightly roached backed appearance. Hence the "low set" tail so often spoke of.

The hip should be broad. A broad hip will carry with it a broad loin and permits a large surface for the attachments of the gluteal and the biceps femoris muscles, the biggest drivers in the power train.

The femur thigh bone should be shorter than the tibia, or lower leg bone. This means that the stifle joint will be in the upper one-third of the hind leg. It is not uncommon to see dogs with a low stifle. They are usually impressively muscled because of the bigger biceps femoris, but are surprisingly weak and slow on the back legs because of the leverage lost by the long thigh. A short femur and long tibia usually means a well bent stifle, which in turn leads to a well bent hock. This last is a really critical aspect of wrestling ability. When a dog finds himself being driven backward, he must rely on the natural springiness of the well bent hock and stifle to control his movement. Dogs with straight or the frequently seen "double jointed" hock of many of the Dibo bred dogs, will wrestle well as long as muscle power can sustain them, but if pushed, will tire in the back end more quickly and soon lose their wrestling ability.

Thirdly, look at the front end. He should have a deep rib cage, well sprung at the top but tapering to the bottom. Deep and elliptical, almost narrow is preferred to the round and barrel chest. The rib cage houses the lungs which are not storage tanks, but pumps. The ribs are like a bellows. Their efficiency is related to the difference in volume between contraction and expansion. A barrel chested dog, in addition to carrying more weight for his height, has an air pump with a short stroke. He must take more breaths to get the same volume of air. Depth of rib cage gives more room for large lungs.

Shoulders should be a little wider than the rib cage at the eighth rib. Too narrow a shoulder does not support adequate musculature but too wide a shoulder makes a dog slow and adds unnecessary weight. The scapula (shoulder blade) should be at a 45 degree or less slope to the ground and broad and flat. The humerus should be at an equal angle in the opposite direction and long enough that the elbow comes below the bottom of the rib cage. The elbows should lie flat, the humerus running almost parallel to the spine; not out at the elbows which gives a wide "English Bulldog" stance. This type of shoulder is more easily dislocated or broken.

The forearm should be only slightly longer than the humerus and heavy and solid—nearly twice the thickness of the metatarsal bones at the hock. The front legs and shoulders must be capable of sustaining tremendous punishment and heaviness can be an asset here.

The relationship between front legs and back should be, at first appearance, of a heavy front and a delicate back. This is because in an athletic dog, the metatarsal bones, hock and lower part of the tibia will be light, fine and springy. The front legs will be heavy and solid looking. The experienced Bulldog man however, will note the wide hip, loin and powerful thigh which makes the back end the most muscular.

The head varies more in the present day Pit Bull. More than any other part of the body, probably because its conformation has the least to do with whether he wins or loses. However, there are certain attributes which appear to be of advantage. First its overall size. Too big a head simply carries more weight and increases the chances of having to fight a bigger dog. Too small a head is easily punished by a nose fighter and is especially easy for an ear fighter to shake. In an otherwise well proportioned dog, the head will appear to be about two-thirds the width of the shoulders and about 25 percent wider at the cheeks than the neck at the base of the skull. From the back of the head to the stop, should be about the same distance as from the stop to the tip of the nose. The bridge of the nose should be well developed which will make the area directly under the eyes considerably wider than the head at the base of the ears. Depth from the top of the head to the bottom of the jaw is important. The jaw is closed by the Temporal Fossa muscle exerting pressure on the Coronoid process. The deeper the head at this point (that is, between the zygomatic arch and the angular process of the bottom of the jaw), the more likely the dog is to have leverage advantage both in closing the jaw and in keeping it closed. A straight, box-like muzzle and well developed mandible will not have much to do with the biting power but will endure most punishment. "Lippy" dogs are continually fanging themselves in a fight, which works greatly to their disadvantage. Teeth should meet in the front, but more importantly, the canines or fangs should slip tightly together, the upper behind the lower when the mouth is closed. Fangs should be wide at the gumline and taper to the end. Soundness and healthy with none missing. The eye elliptical when viewed from the front, triangular when viewed from the side, small and deep set.

In general, such a head will be wedge shaped when viewed either from the top or side, round when viewed from the front.

Skin should be thick and loose, but not in folds. It should appear to fit the dog tightly except around the neck and chest. Here the skin should be loose enough to show vertical folds even in a well conditioned dog.

Sabrina's Candy Kane in a semiformal pose.

The set of the tail is most important. It should be low. The length should come just above the point of the hock, thick at the base and tapering to a point at the end and should hang down like a pump handle when relaxed.

The feet should be small and set high on the pasterns. The gait of the dog should be light and springy.

Most of the above relates to skeletal features of the dog. When we look at muscles, from the breeder's standpoint, it is much more important to look at the genetic features of musculature than those features due to conditioning. A genetically powerful dog can be a winner in the hands of even an inept owner, but a genetically weak dog needs a good matchmaker to win. Conditioning won't do much for him. Think of bones as levers, with the joints as the fulcrum and the muscles being applied to the power source. The power being applied to the lever is more effective the farther away from the fulcrum it is applied. Muscles should be long, with attachments deep down on the bone, well past the joint. Short muscled dogs are impressive looking but not athletic. A muscle's power value lies in its ability to contract. The greater the difference between its relaxed state and its contracted state, the greater the power.

The coat of the dog can be any color or any combination of colors. It should be short and bristled. The gloss of the coat usually reflects the health of the dog and is important to an athletic American Pit Bull Terrier.

Above all, the American Pit Bull Terrier is an all around athlete. His body is called on for speed, power, ability and stamina. He must be balanced in all directions. Too much of one thing robs him of another. He is not an entity formed according to human specialists. In his winning form he is a fighting machine…a thing of beauty.

In judging the American Pit Bull Terrier 100 points will be possible for the ideal dog. The breakdown is as follows:

Overall appearance ....**20 points**
    height-to-weight ratio
    overall body shape
    health of dog

Attitude of dog ....**10 points**
    alertness
    carriage of dog

Head and neck...**15 points**
    teeth
    eyes
    size and shape of head and neck

Front end of dog...**20 points**
    ribs
    shoulders
    chest
    front legs

Back end of dog..**30 points**
    loin
    hip
    stifle

    hock
    back legs and feet
    set of tail

Tail and coat ....**5 points**
    length and shape of tail
    gloss and length of coat

Total   **100 points**

CHAPTER FOUR

Is the American Pit Bull Terrier the Right Dog for Me?

Contrary to the words of the popular song, money can buy you love—if you use the money to buy a dog. Dogs aren't hesitant about making a commitment and never ask you to sign legal papers before promising to love, honor and protect you for the rest of their lives. Having a dog might even make you healthier. Medical science recently proved that close contact with a pet helps people relax and may even lower their blood pressure. Besides, it gives you an incentive to enjoy long walks on lovely days.

SHARING YOUR LIFE WITH A DOG

Acquiring a dog usually enhances a person's life, but for some people, a dog is nothing more than a burdensome responsibility. Sometimes the timing is wrong. A person who would enjoy a dog a couple of years down the line may become impatient and acquire his or her dog too soon.

Before determining if a Pit Bull is your dream dog, it's important to decide whether owning any dog fits into your life right now. Try to do the following self-analysis in private, not while visiting a breeder and hugging a beautiful puppy. In a dispute between love and logic, we all know which one will win.

Among the questions you should ask yourself before acquiring any dog are:

1. Is a dog what I really want, or am I just restless or bored right now and need a change?

Dogs purchased simply to satisfy a nagging discontent are often ignored once their newness and puppy cuteness wears off. This is heartbreaking and incredibly unfair to a loyal pet. Healthy dogs can live ten years or more, so before buying a dog, make sure you want one for its entire life, not just for a brief period of entertainment.

2. Do I have enough time to give my dog attention, training and exercise?

A Pit Bull can be your dream dog if you choose carefully and know what you're getting into. This is Virginia Isaac with Fonseca's HK Az. Lady (Monkey), whose pedigree can be traced back 104 years.

Puppies need lots of attention to become the happy, well-trained dogs you want them to be.

A new puppy or dog will need more of your time during your first few months together than it will later, but even adult dogs need to socialize with people, and review their training and exercise daily. You may have time on your hands and wish those hands were petting a puppy, but think ahead before buying a dog. Are you a college student? Rentals near universities often accept pets, but once you enter the job market it may be difficult to find a suitable rental that allows dogs. Do you have a challenging career? If so, could climbing the corporate ladder also mean moving frequently, or working such long hours that a dog waiting at the door would become a burden rather than a blessing? Is having a family in your future? If so, will you have the time and energy to tend your baby without discarding your dog?

3. Can I afford a dog?

The initial price of a puppy is not the only cost you should consider. In fact, it's wise to purchase the finest puppy you can afford, as a well-bred, healthy, puppy often costs less in the long run. All dogs need food, annual vaccinations, regular worming, a program of heartworm prevention and a secure area for exercise. In addition, they need veterinary care when they are sick or hurt. Other expenses include a collar and leash, food and water dishes, toys and, usually, spaying or neutering. Ask yourself if you could afford emergency treatment for your dog if it broke its leg. If your dog's accident would put you on a budget of beans for a month, and that's okay with you (and the rest of your family), then go ahead and purchase your puppy. Just have your priorities in order first.

4. Will a dog fit into my home and my lifestyle?

The size and location of your home, your spouse's feelings, your children's ages, your hobbies and your activity level are all important considerations when deciding whether to make a dog part of your family.

If you're vice president of the local antique collectors association, or you dream of seeing your home showcased in a magazine, think hard before buying a puppy. That doesn't mean you shouldn't have a dog at all. You might derive maximum enjoyment and minimum anxiety from an already well-trained adult dog. Do you travel often? Once you are a dog owner, you will either have to locate motels that accept dogs, or find a trusted establishment where you can board your pet.

PERSONALITY TRAITS OF SUCCESSFUL AMERICAN PIT BULL TERRIER OWNERS

Once you decide to get a dog, it's matchmaking time. If you've read this far, the American Pit Bull Terrier is obviously on your list of possible choices. The Pit Bull certainly is a superb dog, but it is absolutely not the ideal dog for everyone. Pit Bull owners are individualists, but those who have successfully owned the breed for years have a few traits in common. The Pit Bull could be your dream dog if many of the personality traits listed here fit you. But if few of these traits sound like you, think long and hard before purchasing an APBT. There are more than two hundred other registered breeds of dogs in the United States to choose from.

American Pit Bull Terrier owners often have:

1. A strong sense of humor.
2. A bit of the child in them, no matter what their age.

3. A moderate to high activity level.
4. A reasonable degree of fitness.
5. Experience in dog training (or a willingness to learn).
6. The know-how to combine patience with persistence.
7. A sense of responsibility about keeping their pets confined to their own property.
8. A special love for precocious animals, even though they may present more of a training challenge than dogs of lesser intelligence.
9. Respect and understanding of the Pit Bull's raw potential.
10. A preference for exuberant dogs over placid types.
11. The self-confidence to politely ignore rude comments from strangers.
12. An eye that finds beauty in short-coated animals of massive musculature.

In addition, good owners of American Pit Bull Terriers are able to handle their dogs. The general rule of dog strength is that a dog is approximately as strong as a human three times its weight. That means a sixty-pound dog is as strong as a 180-pound man. Since the Pit Bull is the strongest dog in the world for its size, a sixty-pounder would be comparable to a 180-pound professional athlete in top form, not a 180-pound office worker who spends evenings and weekends watching television.

Larry Jenkins, Starfire's "granddad," makes a point of visiting his favorite girl as often as possible.

Does that mean only muscle-men should own Pit Bulls? No way. Well-trained APBTs are often beautifully handled by children. What's important is that the APBT be well trained, and successful owners know this and are willing to take on the responsibility and joy of training their dog. If the dog will be handled by a child, the child should also understand the basics of training.

Pit Bull owners who are blessed with high spirits and the joy of living get the most pleasure from the breed. The American Pit Bull Terrier still wants to frolic long after its muzzle turns gray, and most confirmed owners enjoy playing with their dogs. In fact, many people consider the breed's perennial puppyness an endearing plus.

Many Pit Bull owners are enthusiastic, competitive or both. Since the breed shares its owner's enthusiasm and excels in the show ring, obedience competition, weight pulling, agility and Schutzhund, many exciting sports are available. Owners who have enthusiasm but don't want to become involved in weekend competitions may find volunteer work with a pet therapy group very fulfilling. Descriptions of these activities appear in chapter 9.

No dog should be allowed to run loose, but safe confinement is exceptionally important when owning a Pit Bull. Out and about without human guidance, the Pit Bull may get into trouble with another dog. Successful APBT owners have a strong sense of responsibility to their breed and their neighbors, and buy or build whatever it takes to keep their dog on their own property. Sometimes it takes a lot. Pit Bulls can dig like badgers, and a few them can clear seven-foot fences from a standstill.

HOUSING AN AMERICAN PIT BULL TERRIER

The closer you and your dog live together, the closer the bond between you becomes. House dogs, provided they get sufficient exercise, are the luckiest dogs of all. Dogs are social animals and suffer loneliness and boredom when confined to quarters away from human contact. Exceptions to this are kennel dogs whose owners set aside a chunk of time every day for training, playing and petting, not just a brief visit at feeding time.

Those lucky Pit Bulls that share the family home should still have a crate. Discussed in detail in chapter 6, a dog crate will maintain its usefulness during your dog's entire life. It can serve as a home within the home, and is useful for confining Delilah when she is damp from a bath, in season or has muddy feet. It can also be used to rescue Dee when your cousin visits and her active toddler persists in teasing her. Someday it might even save the evening when a client comes to dinner and it turns out that he is terrified of dogs.

Where a house dog sleeps depends on where you want it to sleep. Allowed free choice, Delilah will probably end up in bed with you or one of your children. If such accommodations don't suit you, teach her that beds are off limits. Dee's second choice will be the sofa or easy chair, but dogs are creatures of habit and can be trained to stay off the furniture if that's what you want. Suitable sleeping arrangements might be a soft pad beside your bed, a doggie bed in your daughter's room, the living room rug, a crate in the kitchen or a throw rug near the back door.

THE OUTDOOR DOG

If your Pit Bull will be an outside dog or will spend part of the day outdoors, it's vital that it have adequate shelter from heat, rain and cold, and that it be securely confined to your property.

Where should you put your outside dog's shelter and exercise area? Just as close to the house as possible. Close enough so you can pat Beau when you leave the house, and enjoy his welcome when you return. Close enough so Johnny has time to say good-bye to Beau before he leaves for school. Close enough so you can talk to Beau while you weed around the tomato plants. Close enough so that visiting Beau is a frequent pleasure, not a once-a-day chore.

If Beau will be outside only when you are away, the location of his outdoor area isn't as important, since he will be in the house with you part of every day. But his outside shelter should still give protection from the elements, and the area must be escape-proof. The following are several possibilities for safe, outdoor confinement.

The Fenced Yard

A high, well-installed chain-link fence is sufficient for most (but not all) Pit Bulls. Keep a careful eye on the condition of your fence, especially around the bottom where Beau may try to dig his way out, and watch to see if Beau develops exceptional jumping ability. If you already have a chain-link or equally secure fenced yard, perhaps all Beau needs is a cozy doghouse.

The Dog Run

A high chain-link kennel run with a wire roof and a doghouse at one end should keep Beau where he belongs even if he grows into an Olympic-quality jumper. Burying the chain link six inches underground and anchoring it in cement will stop Beau from making like a gopher. Shade screen over the wire roof and down one or two sides of the run will help cool the area. A corrugated fiberglass roof is also excellent. It will protect Beau from rain and snow, and, in certain colors, will reflect the sun's rays.

Make sure your Pit Bull is in a securely fenced yard while he's outside and out of your supervision.

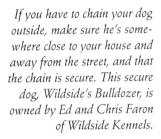

If you have to chain your dog outside, make sure he's somewhere close to your house and away from the street, and that the chain is secure. This secure dog, Wildside's Bulldozer, is owned by Ed and Chris Faron of Wildside Kennels.

Patio blocks, or cement finished to a rough surface, make good, easily cleaned flooring for the pen. Pea gravel is another good flooring material, but it is a little harder to clean and has to be replaced occasionally. However, gravel is better for Beau's feet than cement or patio blocks.

Plan before you build. It's often possible to save money by using one wall of your house or garage as one side of the pen.

The Chain

Chances are that Pit Bulls have been raised on chains more than any other way, but this method of confinement has many disadvantages. One disadvantage to chaining Beau is that he can become a target for teasing and tormenting by neighbors, and his temperament may be altered as a result of this stress. Another is that someone could let him loose, or even steal him. Also, no matter how nice a dog Beau is, you could still be sued by the parents of a child who played with him on your property without your permission, and was scratched by his dewclaw, or bruised by becoming tangled in the chain.

Sometimes there is no alternative, so if you must chain Beau, pick a place as close to your house and as invisible from the street as possible, and make sure the chain, the swivel, the collar and all the connections are extremely sturdy and in good working order.

The Doghouse

Many pet supply stores have excellent doghouses for sale, or you can make one yourself. There are only a few requirements to building a good doghouse.

The floor of Beau's house should be raised off the ground two or three inches to protect it from rain, snow, dampness and morning dew. A removable roof, or one on hinges, will make it easier to clean the inside. The door should be to one side of the house and partitioned off, with the sleeping space on the side away from the drafty door. To conserve body heat, the sleeping space should be cozy; just the right size for Beau to curl up in comfortably.

The very best bedding is cedar chips. They smell wonderful, stay clean and dry for a long time and help Beau keep cool in summer and warm in winter. If you can't find cedar bedding, wood shavings are a dependable second choice. Make the bedding deep, especially in winter. When the weather isn't too cold, another good choice is indoor/outdoor carpeting. Buy two pieces of carpet so you have a replacement when you shampoo one of them.

Neither straw nor newspaper make good outdoor bedding, as they don't dry out well once they become wet. Also, damp newsprint will rub off on Beau's coat, dulling its shine and turning his white markings gray.

THE FREEDOM FANTASY

Some dog owners think they are doing an injustice to their dog unless they let it experience freedom. In fact, seven million dogs die every year due to accidents encountered while roaming free. Besides being killed by cars, loose dogs eat poisonous substances, get picked up by animal control officers and can be a menace to livestock, cats, the neighbor's flower bed and other dogs. Seven million is a lot of dead dogs, and putting yours in a position to become a statistic isn't doing it a favor. Beau is a domestic animal. Instead of freedom, give him what he really wants: your companionship.

CHAPTER FIVE

Picking the Ultimate American Pit Bull Terrier

Outside of marriage, acquiring a dog may be your only opportunity to actually choose a member of your family.

The first step in finding a fabulous four-legged family member is to locate a reputable breeder. Such a breeder usually specializes in the American Pit Bull Terrier and has devoted years to preserving and improving the breed. He or she probably has a couple to several excellent dogs and may even exhibit at dog shows.

Most reliable breeders treasure their dogs as a hobby, not a business, and are usually pleased and proud to show you their kennel and the dam (mother) of the pups, and sometimes the sire (father) as well. But don't be surprised if the sire isn't there. Part of breeding for excellence is studying dogs and pedigrees to find the very best match for the brood bitch. If that special stud dog lives at the other end of the country, a good breeder will find a way to get the bitch to him (usually shipping by plane), and will pay a fee (or possibly a puppy) for his "service." Chances are, if the sire is not on the premises the breeder will be able to show you his picture and pedigree. You may even have the opportunity to visit with other mature dogs that are closely related to the puppy you are considering.

Good breeders are concerned about the welfare of their puppies, so don't be surprised if the breeder asks you questions about your past history of dog ownership and why you are interested in this breed. Breeders may also inquire about your lifestyle, wondering how much time you spend at home, the ages of your children and if you have a fenced yard. Answer honestly, and don't be insulted. The breeder is just making sure the puppy will have a secure, safe and loving home.

There is something you should make sure of, too, so when you contact a breeder, always ask what qualities he or she breeds for. A variety of answers are acceptable, such as winning shows, good bone, intelligence and correct bites—but either good temperament or good disposition should always be included in the answer.

One way to find Pit Bull breeders is to attend a United Kennel Club (UKC) or American Dog Breeders Association (ADBA) dog show. There you can talk to exhibitors who are showing their dogs. Many of them are actually breeders, and those who aren't will be able to tell you how to find the breeders they respect. Dog shows are fun and educational, even if you have no interest in showing your own dog. At a show you'll see many different dogs of the same breed, and this can help you decide what you really want in an American Pit Bull Terrier.

Another way to locate breeders is to write to the United Kennel Club, 100 Kilgore Road, Kalamazoo, MI 49001-5596, or the American Dog Breeders Association, P.O. Box 1771, Salt Lake City, Utah 84110, and ask about purchasing a recent copy of their magazines. The UKC's magazine, *Bloodlines*, is published bimonthly and ADBA has a quarterly publication called *American Pit Bull Terrier Gazette*. Both publications contain many ads for American Pit Bull Terrier kennels and puppies.

A litter of six-week-old pups frolics on the grass. It's tough to choose when they all look so cute.

Ads for American Pit Bull Terriers also appear in dog publications that are available on newsstands and in animal supply stores. The most popular are *Dog Fancy*, *Dogs USA* and *Dog World*.

The classified section of your local newspaper may also have ads for Pit Bull puppies. Puppy sellers who advertise only in the paper, and not through the dog journals, are often folks who simply bred their Pit Bull to their friend's Pit Bull. While the puppies may make delightful pets, it's a good idea to have plenty of knowledge about the breed before selecting a puppy from this type of litter. This is especially important if you plan to show your dog, as a casual breeder may not be able to help you select a puppy with the potential to win at shows.

After you have located a few breeders with puppies that interest you, the next step is to contact them by phone or letter. Before calling or writing, it's a good idea to make a list of what you want in a puppy so you remember to include it in your conversation or letter. Tell the breeder if you want a male or a female, what colors you like best, and what your expectations are for the dog. These may include whether it will be a family companion; a child's playmate; a guardian; a show dog in conformation classes, obedience or both; an agility prospect; a jogging partner; a camping or fishing buddy; a weight-pulling competitor; or any combination of these. Also tell the breeder if you are going to have the dog spayed or neutered, or if you plan to breed the dog at maturity. A complete list of what you prefer is especially important if you are purchasing your puppy sight-unseen from a distant kennel. The more the breeder learns about what you want, the better selection he or she will be able to make for you.

If you are lucky enough to live within visiting distance of breeders whose puppies interest you, call for appointments instead of arriving unannounced. The majority of hobby breeders have their kennel on the same property as their home, rather than housing their dogs in a separate commercial facility. Most of them are proud to display their dogs and are happy to answer questions, provided you arrive at their convenience.

It's not just pleasant, but actually important that you like and respect the breeder. He or she should be someone you would feel comfortable calling upon later for advice about your dog's health or training. So if you have a bad feeling about the breeder, any of the dogs or the facility, trust your intuition and look elsewhere for a puppy.

PICK OF THE LITTER

Everyone wants it, but it's a different puppy to different people. To someone who shows dogs in conformation competition, the pick is the puppy that comes closest to the description in the breed standard. To the woman who lives alone in the city,

The pick is the puppy that appeals to you, provided it has the temperament to happily share your lifestyle. This confident pup is five weeks old.

the pick is the puppy that alerts instantly to strange sounds. To the couple with three lively sons, the pick is the puppy with the cheerful, devil-may-care disposition that will enjoy the noisy, spirited games of young boys. The pick is the puppy that appeals to you, provided it has the temperament to happily share your lifestyle. Sometimes the last puppy in an excellent litter is far superior in disposition, appearance and health to the best puppy in a mediocre litter. In any case, if you insist on first choice, let the breeder know that up front and expect to pay more for your puppy.

Whether you decide to pick your own puppy or ask the breeder to help you choose one, the following suggestions should help you on selection day.

FEATURES OF A FINE PUPPY

- Did a certain puppy catch your eye immediately? Do you keep going back to that one no matter how hard you try to give each puppy equal time? Are you already naming it in your mind? Trust your instincts. Love at first sight can last a lifetime provided the object of your affection is healthy and has a good disposition.

- Watch the litter play with each other without human interference. The best pet is usually a puppy in the middle of the pecking order—neither the bully nor the scaredy-cat. If you happen to see a puppy stand up to the bully, back the bully off, then go about its business peacefully, pay special attention to that one as it has strong character.

- Look at the puppy's eyes. They should be clear, bright and alert.

- Stroke and examine the puppy's coat. It should be smooth to the touch and glossy.

- Hold the puppy gently but firmly in your hands. Its body should feel solid and substantial.

- Look at the puppy's legs and feet. The legs should appear sturdy enough to easily hold the body and the feet should be compact with the toes close together and arched.

- It's important to see a puppy's reaction to being on a one-to-one basis with you. Ask permission to take the puppies that appeal to you out of sight of their breeder, dam and littermates, one puppy at a time, so you can test their temperaments. Give each puppy a couple of minutes to survey its surroundings, then kneel down and try to induce it to come to you. If it does, pet and praise it, then get up, move away slowly, and see if you can talk the puppy into following you. Show the puppy a doggie toy or a small ball, then roll it on the ground away from (not toward) the puppy. Is the puppy interested? Roll the toy three times to give the puppy time to understand the game. Does it chase or examine the toy, perhaps even pick it up in its mouth and carry it toward you?

- Wait until the puppy is looking away from you, then blow a loud whistle or drop a metal pan about ten feet away from it. Watch the pup's reaction. After being startled, it should recover quickly.

- Pick up that appealing puppy and cradle it securely in your arms. It may struggle briefly, but does it soon relax and enjoy? Does it try to lick you? These are signs of a good disposition. (When lifting a puppy, place one hand under its chest with your forefinger between its front legs and cradle its bottom in your other hand. Being lifted by the front legs is painful and can cause permanent injury to a puppy's shoulders.)

- If the puppy you initially fell for is not interested in playing with you, ask the breeder to tell you how the puppy usually behaves. Young puppies tire easily and it's possible your visit coincided with the pup's nap time. Even the healthiest, happiest pups become limp as dish rags when it's snooze time, and snoozes are sudden and frequent when puppies are young. If the breeder tells you that Sleepy Sal usually behaves like Animated Annie, make arrangements to visit at a different time of day before making your selection.

- If you are planning a show career for your puppy, make sure its teeth have a scissors bite (the upper front teeth should meet tightly outside the lower front teeth). Also watch it move toward you and away from you. Gait is mighty hard to evaluate in a young pup, but you can make sure that its front legs are moving parallel with each other as the puppy comes toward you and that the rear legs are parallel with each other as it moves away. When selecting a show dog, be certain to study the breed standard first. Show dogs are judged by how closely their form matches the ideal conformation described in the standard.

- No matter how beautiful a puppy is, make sure there is some chemistry between you. The first couple of months of puppy ownership are a period of adjustment for both of you, but a puppy that makes you feel good just looking at it will make all the adjustments seem minor.

FEATURES TO FRET OVER

- When you look at or play with the puppy, how do you feel? Excited? Elated? Is this the pal you were looking for? If not, don't buy the puppy just because it is inexpensive, or because buying now is easier than traveling to a few more kennels. The purchase price is only a tiny part of what you will spend on your dog during its lifetime, so be sure you want the dog you get.
- Never purchase a puppy out of pity. When a lively litter of puppies vies for your attention while Shy Sue hides in the corner, don't convince yourself that someone must have been mean to poor Susie. If anyone abused the puppies, more than one of them would show signs of stress. Sue's shyness indicates a temperament problem, and its possible that there isn't enough love in the world, let alone in your household, to turn Sue into a well-adjusted family member.

Determine whether a puppy is shy or simply independent. Don't be tempted to feel sorry for the shy guy; he may have a temperament problem.

Examine a puppy's belly for pimples or raw patches. This one, asleep under a rose bush, has a lovely belly.

- Watch the litter play together and avoid both the bully and any puppy that shies away from its littermates' games.
- Gently grasp the base of the puppy's tail between your thumb, index and middle fingers and run your fingers down the tail from base to tip. Don't buy a puppy with a kink in its tail. The tail is simply an extension of the spinal column, so a bent tail could be a sign of skeletal problems.
- Look at the puppy's belly and question the breeder about any pimples or raw patches.
- Look at the puppy's feet. Don't buy the puppy if the toes are flat and spread apart (splayed), as that type of foot is weak and easily injured.
- When you take a puppy out of sight of its littermates and breeder, it should get its bearings in the new area within a couple of minutes and then show some interest in its surroundings as well as a desire to spend time with you. Avoid any puppy that crouches fearfully in one spot or that runs away.
- Pick up the puppy and cradle it securely in your arms. Does it struggle and/or cry continuously? Does it stiffen with fright and refuse to relax? These are signs of a poor temperament.

- If dog shows are in your puppy's future, stay away from pups that have exceptionally long or thin bodies or legs.
- Don't pick an orphaned puppy or a single puppy with no littermates. To be properly socialized, puppies need to spend a minimum of six weeks, preferably seven, with their mother, brothers and sisters. If you select a puppy under six weeks old, the breeder should be willing to let it stay with its canine family until it is at least forty-two days of age.

HEALTH AND MEDICAL RECORDS

When you take your puppy home, ask the breeder for its feeding, worming and inoculation schedule. Give the worming and inoculation information to your veterinarian so he or she can schedule future treatments. For your puppy's safety, all its inoculations should be up to date before you take it on walks or outings where it may encounter other dogs. Since this may vary depending on where you live, your veterinarian is the best judge of when your puppy may safely travel with you.

ACQUIRING THE ULTIMATE ADULT

Pit Bull puppies are precious. They feel warm and sturdy in your arms. They wear disarming expressions while their antics elicit smiles and laughter. They are vigorous and fun-loving. What's more, when you see your puppy's little tail wagging its entire body, you know it's always delighted to see you. But ask yourself if you will always be delighted to see your pup. Will you (or a family member) be available to tend your pup every time it needs someone?

Young puppies need to be fed four times a day. Like babies, they potty often, eat sloppily and sleep a lot, but not always on your schedule. If not properly supervised, they may teethe on the furniture. Puppies are delightful and learn quickly, but only if their owners are consistent about taking the time to teach them.

Some people have plenty of time to enjoy a dog, but not on the regular, every-few-hour schedule necessary to care for and housebreak a puppy. Other people wish they had a dog, but are hesitant because they don't want to take on the teething and housebreaking stages. There is a remedy for their doglessness: It could be a charming adult Pit Bull.

While not all adult dogs are housebroken, and unsupervised young adults may still gnaw the furniture, mature animals have bigger bladders and longer attention spans than puppies, so they usually learn quite quickly. In addition, adult dogs often take on the family guardian role within a few weeks of entering a loving home, while puppies seldom act as guardians until they are between seven and thirteen months old.

There are many reasons an adult Pit Bull may be available for a new home. Possibilities include death or divorce of the owner; a corporate move with no-pets-allowed housing available; a breeder who doesn't breed females past a certain age or simply no longer needs the dog for breeding; a show dog that became incapable of winning shows for reasons that have no effect on its ability to be a terrific pet; or a dog that was lost or abandoned and is up for adoption. Whatever the reason, it's important you know what it is, because you don't want to be the next person trying to find a home for an unmanageable dog.

Besides skipping the puppy stages, other advantages of acquiring an adult Pit Bull are that you already know exactly how the dog looks and you can tell a great deal about its personality. It's a lot like selecting a puppy, but without some of the guesswork.

Selecting an Adult

Pet and play with the adult Pit Bull to check for mental stability and a willingness to please. Is it loving and attentive or excitable and independent? Is it eager to frolic with you, or is it fearful or aggressive?

Look for character, intelligence, trainability and a sense of humor in an adult Pit Bull. All these dogs have passed a temperament test and are trained for some type of work or competition.

Most important of all, the chemistry should be there. Do you automatically smile when you see the dog? Is the dog happy to see you and content in your company? Is this the dog you want beside you as a constant companion?

Look at the dog's eyes, feet, coat, skin and movement to check for general health. The eyes should be bright, the toes close together and arched, the coat shiny with no splotches of missing hair, the skin smooth and the movement fluid and easy.

Put a leash on the dog and take it for a walk. Does it notice which direction you turn and go your way, or does it choose the direction and stretch your arm hauling you down the street? If the dog is pulling, don't give up on it right away. Perhaps no one ever trained it to walk nicely.

To get an idea whether the dog will easily accept you as leader and learn to walk with you, put the dog on a six-foot lead. Hold the loop of the lead tightly against your waist with both hands and start walking without talking to the dog. After a few steps, change directions quickly and silently by making a sudden right turn. If the dog is momentarily yanked off balance, so much the better. Keep moving, and eight or ten steps later, make another right turn. If the dog catches on and starts to watch where you go and keep up with you, praise it and keep going. Repeat the test continuously for two minutes by walking about eight to ten steps and then suddenly making a right turn. When you stop, ask yourself: Has the dog learned anything? Have you learned anything about the dog?

While parents can select a puppy and bring it home as a present for their children, an adult dog should never be a surprise. Something in the dog's past may cause it to fear men, dislike children or behave aggressively toward women, so every member of the family should meet the dog before a decision is made.

Finding an adult Pit Bull is much the same as shopping for a puppy. The best first bet is checking with breeders. Also, contact the local American Pit Bull Terrier club if there is one in your area. The magazines mentioned earlier as sources of puppy and kennel ads are also useful for locating mature dogs.

IS BOWSER A BLUE BLOOD?

Every dog has a pedigree, but not every dog is a purebreed. A pedigree is simply a list of ancestors, just like a family tree. For example, one of your grandparents may be Australian, another Irish, another French and the fourth British, but you still have a family tree. Along the same line, a dog's four grandparents may be a Labrador Retriever, an Irish Setter, a Pit Bull and a Pointer, and that is the dog's family tree. The dog has a pedigree, but he certainly isn't a purebreed. Generally, when you see an ad for "pedigreed puppies," the seller really means purebred puppies and is guilty only of improper usage of the

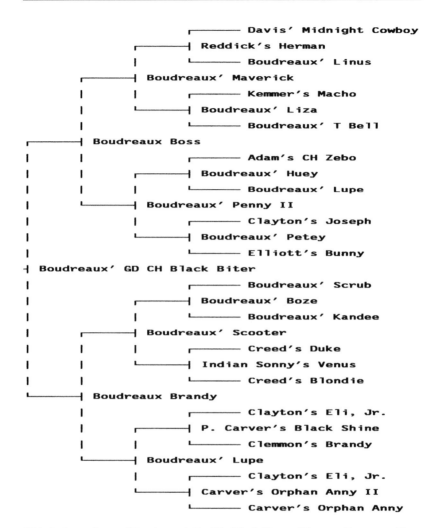

```
                                    ┌───────── Davis' Midnight Cowboy
                        ┌──────────┤ Reddick's Herman
                        │           └───────── Boudreaux' Linus
            ┌──────────┤ Boudreaux' Maverick
            │           │           ┌───────── Kemmer's Macho
            │           │ ┌─────────┤ Boudreaux' Liza
            │           └─┤          └───────── Boudreaux' T Bell
┌──────────┤ Boudreaux Boss
│           │                        ┌───────── Adam's CH Zebo
│           │            ┌──────────┤ Boudreaux' Huey
│           │            │           └───────── Boudreaux' Lupe
│           └───────────┤ Boudreaux' Penny II
│                        │           ┌───────── Clayton's Joseph
│                        └──────────┤ Boudreaux' Petey
│                                    └───────── Elliott's Bunny
┤ Boudreaux' GD CH Black Biter
│                                    ┌───────── Boudreaux' Scrub
│                        ┌──────────┤ Boudreaux' Boze
│                        │           └───────── Boudreaux' Kandee
│           ┌───────────┤ Boudreaux' Scooter
│           │            │           ┌───────── Creed's Duke
│           │            └──────────┤ Indian Sonny's Venus
│           │                        └───────── Creed's Blondie
└──────────┤ Boudreaux Brandy
            │                        ┌───────── Clayton's Eli, Jr.
            │            ┌──────────┤ P. Carver's Black Shine
            │            │           └───────── Clemmon's Brandy
            └───────────┤ Boudreaux' Lupe
                         │           ┌───────── Clayton's Eli, Jr.
                         └──────────┤ Carver's Orphan Anny II
                                     └───────── Carver's Orphan Anny
```

This is the pedigree of Boudreaux' Gr. Ch. Black Biter, a Therapy Dog owned by Wanda Frazier. He's the dog in the middle of the form. Follow the line up and down to Boudreaux Boss and Boudreaux Brandy. Boss is Biter's sire and Brandy is his dam. Now follow the lines up and down from Boudreaux Boss to his sire, Buodreaux' Maverick and dam, Boudreaux' Penny II. They are Biter's grandsire and granddam on his sire's side. Do the same for Boudreaux Brandy and you will find Biter's grandsire and granddam on his dam's side. This is a four-generation pedigree, so you can go all the way back to Black Biter's great-great-grandsires and great-great-granddams.

word "pedigreed." But just in case, ask to see ADBA or UKC registration certificates before falling for a puppy from that litter.

A purebred dog is descended from dogs that were all of the same breed. That means a purebred American Pit Bull Terrier's parents, grandparents and great-grandparents were all American Pit Bull Terriers, and so on, as far back as records were kept.

Pedigrees can tell you more than just the names of a dog's ancestors. If any of those ancestors won a title, its abbreviation will appear as part of the dog's name on the pedigree. For example, if an ancestor earned a championship, the letters "Ch." will appear before its name. If it won an obedience title, such as Companion Dog, the abbreviation "U-CD" will follow the dog's name on the pedigree. From studying a dog's pedigree you will discover if the dog was linebred on one particularly great ancestor, or if it is the result of a backcross, an outcross or inbreeding (see chapter 10 for details).

No matter how outstanding it appears, remember that a pedigree is only as impressive as the dog it represents. A quality dog with a quality pedigree is a treasure, but an inferior dog with a magnificent pedigree is still an inferior dog.

So, is Bowser a blue blood? When Bowser is ADBA or UKC registered, and your name appears as owner on his registration certificate, Bowser is a true canine blue blood—a registered American Pit Bull Terrier.

REGISTERING YOUR PUREBRED

The American Dog Breeder's Association (ADBA) and the United Kennel Club (UKC) register American Pit Bull Terriers. When you acquire an ADBA-registered puppy, the breeder should give you a light tan registration certificate. Information on this certificate will include a description of your puppy, its birth date, its sire and dam, its breeder and its current owner. Never accept a photocopy of this certificate, as the ADBA must receive the original copy from you in order to register your puppy in your name. If the breeder cannot give you the registration form at the time of purchase, but promises it later, ask for a bill of sale stating that ADBA registration papers will follow. The bill of sale should include the puppy's description, birth date, breeder, sire, dam and registered owner. Without the original tan form, a bill of sale is your only proof that you bought a registered puppy and registration papers were included in the purchase price. It's preferable to obtain the original registration at the time of purchase, and many buyers will not accept a puppy unless its "papers" are available at the same time.

As soon as you receive your puppy's tan ADBA registration form, fill it out on the back and mail it to ADBA with the appropriate fee. At that time you may also have the opportunity to name your dog (in twenty-five letters or less), and you can order its pedigree. Soon ADBA will send you a new registration paper, one with your name listed as owner of the dog.

When you purchase a UKC-registered puppy, it should come with a green puppy registration certificate. The certificate has a bill of sale on the back, which the breeder will transfer to you. You may name your puppy on this paper and are allowed twenty-two letters and spaces to do so. Each name must be a minimum of two words, but if you want your dog to have a one-word name, just use your own last name with it. For example, if you want to call your dog Smoky and your last name is Furman, simply print Furman's Smoky on the form. Again, accept only the original registration certificate or a bill of sale with all appropriate information about the puppy, stating that UKC registration papers are included in the purchase price.

When the dog is named and the registration certificate is filled out, return it to the UKC with the requested fee. Soon you will receive a registration certificate with your dog's name on it and a copy of your dog's pedigree. If your dog's ancestors have been registered with the UKC for three or more generations, your dog will be designated "Purple Ribbon" on its registration certificate. This is the "PR" you often see in kennel ads.

Signature Puppies

Sometimes the kennel where you purchased your pup may want to either name it or include its kennel name as part of your dog's registered name. This is not an unusual request. Breeding for excellence is an art form, and putting a kennel name on a fine dog is like an artist signing his work.

CHAPTER SIX

What Your New Dog Needs

Once you decide that puppy love is in your future, a little advance planning helps you enjoy your new arrival, and keeps it happy and healthy.

PUPPY PROOFING
FOR YOUR FUTURE HOUSE DOG

Until Bear is housebroken and has stopped teething, you'll want to confine him to one easily cleaned room of your home when no one is there to supervise him. If you are raising Bear to be a house dog, the kitchen (if not exceptionally large) or a bathroom is ideal. Basements and garages are too isolated to teach a puppy how to be part of the family.

A wire mesh baby gate (not easily chewed plastic or wood) often works better than a door when confining a young puppy to a room. There seems to be something about the combination of loneliness and a closed door that can lead to incessant barking and destructive behavior (usually aimed at the door). When Bear

The bathroom is a good place to confine your puppy while she learns to be a house dog.

gets big enough to try climbing the baby gate, booby-trap the top. Take a couple of empty soda cans, put half a handful of pennies or gravel inside them, and seal the opening with tape. Then lean them along the top of the gate. When Bear tries to climb, the sound of the cans clattering to the floor may change his mind.

To make the room (and the rest of your home) safe for Bear when he is unsupervised, put all cleaning agents, antifreeze, pesticides and other household, garage or garden chemicals out of his reach. If it isn't possible to eliminate electrical wires that Bear can reach, coat them with Bitter Apple, a safe, evil-tasting substance especially created to prevent chewing. If you have houseplants, identify them and look them up to make sure they aren't poisonous. Many common house plants are. All plants should be placed out of Bear's reach simply because no puppy is able to resist playing with a plant, but extra precautions are necessary with poisonous plants. Even when they are hanging high, they still shed leaves and berries. For example, poinsettia leaves are so toxic that eating just one can kill a small child, and those pretty mistletoe berries are also deadly poison. If you like your nontoxic plants just where they are and you want Bear to learn to leave them alone, spray them with Bitter Apple leaf protector.

Expect an unsupervised puppy to teethe on whatever is reachable, from throw rugs, toilet paper, towels and the shower curtain, to a bag of potatoes if the cupboard door is left ajar. In fact, puppies have been known to chomp on anything from fountain pens to scouring pads. But don't worry. Securing closet and cupboard doors, or flipping the shower curtain up over the rod, isn't so hard to remember once you have your precious puppy.

THE GREAT CRATE

Dogs descended from denning animals that spent a great deal of their time in the relative security of their lair. That's why it will take only a brief period of adjustment before Bear feels comfortable and protected in a dog crate. Contrary to being cruel, as some new dog owners imagine, dog crates have saved dogs' lives and owners' tempers.

Give your puppy things you want him to chew on; most dogs love fleece toys.

Buy baby Bear a crate that is large enough for a grown American Pit Bull Terrier to stand up and turn around in comfortably. The crate will be a tremendous help with housebreaking, because Bear will soon learn not to soil his bed (see Chapter 7 for details). It can also serve as a safe playpen, so Bear can't damage furniture or swallow something dangerous when you are away or asleep. The crate should be placed in Bear's puppy-proofed room, right up front near the baby gate.

When figuring out how to use the room and the crate, think of how parents set up their baby's area. Ideally the baby has a room, which they may refer to as the nursery. In the nursery there is a crib and a playpen, and a car seat is in the closet. The playpen is easily moved to another room of the house if Mom or Dad want baby to play near them safely without demanding their total attention. Visualize Bear's puppy-proofed room as the nursery, and the crate as a combination crib, playpen and car seat, and you'll easily figure out how to use each one for your own convenience.

If it's impossible to give Bear his own puppy-proofed room, you can still enjoy the benefits of a crate. In fact, without the confined area for your puppy, a crate becomes almost essential. Coming home to a safely crated puppy is much nicer for both of you than coming home to a messy rug and teeth marks on the furniture. Also, a securely crated puppy has a better chance of surviving a car accident than a loose puppy does. And if you and Bear are traveling alone, think how much better you will drive without Bear climbing all over you.

Bear's crate should be snug, soft and comfortable inside. The bedding should be easy to clean or change in the event of a mishap, and not dangerous if chewed or swallowed. For example, several thicknesses of newspaper (black and white, not color like the Sunday comics) make good bedding for an indoor crate. For extra coziness, rip one section into long, thin streamers and place them in the crate on top of the whole sections.

Every time you put Bear in his crate, toss a favorite toy or a special treat in the crate ahead of him. Say "crate" and, as gently as possible, put Bear in and shut the door. Then walk away. Don't wait and watch to see how Bear will react, because that

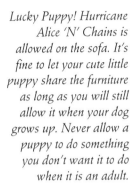

Lucky Puppy! Hurricane Alice 'N' Chains is allowed on the sofa. It's fine to let your cute little puppy share the furniture as long as you will still allow it when your dog grows up. Never allow a puppy to do something you don't want it to do when it is an adult.

will entice him to react. Pretty soon, Bear will learn the word "crate" and enter it himself, without your help.

The crate should never be used as punishment, and it should never be overused. No dog should be forced to spend the majority of its life in its crate. Eventually, Bear's attitude toward his crate should become neutral. If he either hates his crate or loves it too much, something is wrong. Many families leave a crate in a corner, door always open, even after their dogs are grown. Children are taught that when the dog retires to its crate, it is tired and should be left alone. And the dog knows it has a hideaway of its own, where it can take a nap when it needs one.

Bear may cry the first few times he is introduced to his crate, but if you walk away and don't take him out of the crate until he settles down, he'll soon become accustomed to it. If he takes longer than three or four days to stop complaining in his crate, see "Noise Stoppers" in Chapter 7.

SAFE TOYS

Toys are not an extra, but an essential. Bear needs something safe to gnaw on while he is teething, and should have a couple of toys available all the time. Whenever he is placed in his crate, he should be accompanied by a safe toy or two, and toys should also be handy when Bear is out and about, enjoying time with the family.

Bear will still enjoy chewing when he grows up, but he won't be driven to mouth everything in sight the way teething puppies do. Actually, chewing is good for dogs. It helps remove plaque from their teeth and promotes healthy gums.

Rawhide chew toys are a traditional favorite, but there have been rare accidents when a dog ripped a chunk from a rawhide, got it caught in its throat and choked. So give Bear rawhide only when you are home and in the same room with him, and don't choose rawhide for his crate toy.

Squeaky toys (lightweight rubber or plastic with squeakers inside) are popular with pups, but they are only safe when you are either watching or joining in the play. These types of toys are easily torn apart by Pit Bull puppies and then swallowed, dangerous squeaker and all. It's best to keep Bear's squeaky toy out of his reach, then bring it down every few days and enjoy it with him for a few special minutes of fun.

Chew toys made of nylon are safe in Bear's mouth even when you aren't at home. Younger pups prefer the softer, equally safe, gummy-type nylon chews. Solid, hard rubber toys are also safe and fun, but eventually Bear may be able to mangle even those labeled "indestructible." When you see that he is

Candy's Diamond Veronica, owned by Doug Frels, DVM, has been putting her nylon wishbone to good use.

gouging pieces out of his rubber toys, don't leave him alone with them.

The braided rope toys sold at pet supply stores are fun for games of tug, and good for helping to keep Bear's teeth tartar-free. If Bear starts unstringing his rope, don't let him alone with it, as swallowing the strings could cause intestinal problems. For the ultimate treat, buy a sterilized bone toy and stuff it with cheese. That should keep Bear occupied for awhile.

After Bear owns a few toys, don't let him have them all at once. Instead, rotate them every few days, putting different ones in his crate, play area and in the room where the family gathers. That way Bear will be less likely to become bored with his belongings.

PRACTICAL DOG DISHES

Practical dog dishes for food and water are easy to clean and difficult, if not impossible, to tip over. Many companies have designed dishes with these features in mind. Bear should have one dish for food and another for water. The food dish should be washed after each use, and the water dish should be refilled with fresh water frequently and washed thoroughly once a day. When selecting dishes, remember that Bear will grow and so will the size of his meals.

When feeding Bear, place his dish on the floor in such a way that it won't slide across the floor while he is trying to eat. For example, putting it in a corner of the room works well.

It's always best to have your dog eat indoors, but if you feed outside during the warm months, pick up Bear's food dish as soon as he finishes. Otherwise, every bug in the neighborhood will be attracted to Bear's outdoor area. If Bear eats and drinks outside during cold weather, don't use metal dishes, as his tongue could stick to the frozen metal. Even in winter, constant access to fresh water (*not* snow) is critical, so if you won't be home to frequently remove the ice from Bear's water dish, look into buying a self-warming dish.

GROOMING GIZMOS

Unlike hairy breeds, Pit Bulls have easy-to-care-for wash-and-wear coats. All you need to keep Bear beautiful are a brush with short, soft to medium bristles, a toenail clipper, a good quality pH-balanced dog shampoo (sometimes you may need insecticide shampoo or dip) and a soft toothbrush. The rest of Bear's bathing and grooming needs are probably already in your medicine chest (see chapter 8 for a bathing and grooming guide).

The nicest brushes are sometimes called "hound gloves" and are actually a mitten with horse hair or boar bristles on them. When selecting Bear's toenail clipper, make sure it is designated "heavy duty." He'll need it later, as adult Pit Bulls have thick, tough toenails. It's best not to bathe a puppy any more often than you absolutely have to, so you may want to purchase a dry shampoo (one that goes on dry hair and doesn't need rinsing), for spot cleaning baby Bear.

FIRST COLLAR AND LEASH

Wait until you bring Bear home before buying a collar, so you can get one that will fit his neck perfectly. Bear's collar should apply no pressure as it encircles his neck, but it shouldn't be loose enough to slip over his head.

The collar should be flat, made of nylon webbing or leather, and should have a buckle and ring for attaching the leash. Check the fit of Bear's collar weekly. Puppies grow fast, and collars must be replaced immediately when they become too small.

Bear's leash should be five to six feet long and made of leather, nylon webbing or some other strong, flexible fabric. Neither the collar nor the leash should be made of chain. You may want a chain training collar as a teaching aid when Bear is older, but he should wear it only for training, not in place of his regular collar.

POOPER SCOOPER

Available in pet supply stores, poop scoops are convenient for cleaning up your yard. It's also important to clean up after Bear when you take him for walks; in fact, in many places, it's the law. While there are various items on the market for this purpose, many dog owners simply carry a couple of plastic bags with them on their walks. The bags fit in a pocket or purse and may be turned inside-out for the pick-up, then closed and tossed in the nearest garbage can.

AND IN ADDITION

Before bringing Bear home, you will want to have nutritious puppy food in the cupboard and the address and phone number of a trusted veterinarian on hand. See Chapter 8 for more on feeding and veterinary care.

CHAPTER SEVEN

Little Puppy Discovers Big World (Your Guide to Socialization and Training)

Self-confidence is part of the very character of the Pit Bull, but no animal will behave bravely in noisy, new places unless it is accustomed to going on outings and encountering many different sights and sounds. To become cheerful, reliable companions, puppies must be well socialized.

Imagine how a child would react on the first day of school if he had been so overprotected that it was also his first experience outside of his own house and yard. His ordeal would begin with a walk or a drive to the school. On the way, he would see strange houses, stores, animals, billboards and people, and he might even get carsick. On the playground, he wouldn't know how to respond to the group of noisy, excited children. Familiar only with his parents, and perhaps a few relatives who visited, he would be scared of the strange adult called Teacher. The size of the school building would be intimidating, and he may not know how to navigate stairs. Insecure and anxious, he could become defensive and fight off the first child who approached, or simply hide in a corner, too terrified to talk or learn.

Luckily for children, they usually begin going out with their parents at an early age, and are social enough to adjust quickly by the time they enter kindergarten. But puppies aren't always so lucky.

Now imagine the additional dismay our imaginary child would endure if he had experienced only a couple of trips outside the home before the first day of school, and both of those trips had been visits to the doctor for vaccinations. In his young mind, leaving home, entering a different building and seeing a stranger would correlate with pain. And that's exactly what happens to some puppies.

SOCIALIZATION: ESSENTIAL AND ENTERTAINING

Puppies go through critical periods of social development from birth to sixteen weeks of age. During the first six to seven weeks, they learn from their dam (mother) and their littermates (brothers and sisters). From their dam, they learn respect for authority, which leads to a more trainable dog. Playing with their littermates teaches them social interaction and how to moderate aggression. In fact, the wild wrestling sessions enjoyed by Pit Bull pups make them less body- and sound-sensitive, resulting in dogs that are more tolerant of children, loud noises and other dogs.

The ideal time to take a puppy home is when it reaches nine weeks of age. By then it is mentally mature enough to adjust to leaving its dam and littermates, and soon settles into its human family.

To be properly socialized with dogs, puppies need interaction with their dam and littermates until they are between six and seven weeks old. A little time with Mama is good for them even after they are thoroughly weaned, provided Mama is still willing. Here Ch. 'PR' Gaff's CA Hurricane Justice patiently lets a couple of pups interrupt her rest.

Dogs remember all their lives what they learned about the world when they were between seven and sixteen weeks of age. Those nine weeks shape their personality, making them fearless or fearful, outgoing or shy, eager to learn or resentful of training. The brevity of this time period is a throwback to the dog's wild ancestors. It correlates to when wild pups or cubs ventured out of the den for the first time to hastily learn the lessons of survival. Everything had to be instilled in a hurry, because young animals that made a mistake in the wild rarely got a second chance.

Although domesticated for centuries, dogs still arrive in the world programmed to learn how to handle their environment during their first four months of life. With or without their owner's help, they will form perceptions of what is safe and what is dangerous. With their owner's help, they will be introduced to a friendly world and grow up confident and outgoing. Without their owner's help, they will have chance encounters with frightening noises, strangers and scary objects, and may grow up defensive or shy. A Pit Bull, for all its outward toughness, is still a sensitive animal. The amount of attention and socialization it receives as a youngster has an enormous effect on its mental development and its attitude toward life.

The good news is that socializing your Pit Bull puppy is not only easy, but fun. In fact, it may be the only game in town that has only two rules. Rule one is never pet or talk to your pup when it is showing fear. Rule two is always praise your pup for being brave.

The only complication with puppy socialization is that you must have this fun frequently while your pup is between seven and sixteen weeks old. When that critical period of development is over, it can never be recaptured.

Socializing in the Home

Educational toys for human babies sell well because parents know that while their children play, they are also learning how to manipulate and understand their world. Play-learning works

Denise Hanson knows that her puppy, Taylor, should be encouraged for walking properly on the leash and ignored if he acts fearful.

best for young puppies, too, and their games and toys aren't even expensive. For example, human babies learn about noise when they play with rattles and other toys that let them control the volume and duration of the noise. Puppies that learn how to create and stop a racket also become more confident around loud noises.

Constructive Clamor

The best toy for noise conditioning is an empty half-gallon or gallon plastic milk container without a top. It doesn't matter if the container is bigger than Samson because a milk jug is lightweight and can be pulled by the handle. Lay the jug on the floor, and ignoring Samson, turn on the TV or read the paper. Sam may have to overcome an initial fear of this strange object, and might approach it and back off several times. Just ignore the whole scene and eventually he will become brave enough to drag the jug, then shake it and finally bang it against walls and table legs. Like a child with a toy drum, Samson is learning that noise isn't so scary because it can be controlled. Later, he can graduate to a louder toy. Put a few pebbles inside a milk jug and screw the lid on to make a rowdy rattle. But watch carefully when Sam plays with this toy, so he doesn't chew off and swallow the lid.

Savvy Sights

Pups sometimes spook at people who are wearing odd hats, big sunglasses, flapping rain gear or other accessories that change the shape of the human body. To teach Samson that there is just a regular person inside those clothes, raid your closet for rain gear, a couple of hats, boots and anything else that will change your appearance, including Halloween costumes. Get the children involved, as they will enjoy the costume party, but be sure they are old enough to understand the purpose of the game and won't try to frighten baby Samson.

Wildside Tiger Lil, owned by Ed and Chris Faron, cuddles with her nine-week-old son, Wildside's Hellraiser.

Begin with a single item, a wide-brimmed hat or a trench coat, and let Samson watch you put it on. Then call him to you for a pat or a treat. If Sam seems a bit wary of you in a trench coat or hat, get down to his level and pretend to tie your shoe. That gives him an opportunity to check out the scary item up close, without a word from you. Always let Sam reach you and make the first move. Then it's fine to pet him.

When Samson either enjoys or ignores you and your family putting on and taking off silly clothes, have your children (or you) walk in an unusual way wearing a big coat or boots. Shuffle or hop and make funny noises, but sink to the floor and ignore Sam if he seems frightened. Wait to pet him until after he approaches and touches you or your children first. If Sam is a wary puppy, add items gradually. Whatever you do, don't suddenly appear decked out like Dracula, with flapping arms and a swirling cape, or you could crush his confidence instead of cultivating it.

That Tender Touch

If baby Samson allows you to touch every part of his body, it will be easier to care for him when he's sixty pounds of full-grown muscle. Conditioning Sam to be tolerant of touch can lower your blood pressure (petting dogs does that) and help you and him bond to each other. It should be restful and pleasurable for you both.

After a tiring day, collapse in front of the TV with Samson on your lap and pet him while you unwind. This works best if Sam recently had exercise and is also ready to relax. When petting Sam, handle every square inch of him. Touch him from the tip of his nose to the pads of his toes.

If Sam doesn't want to be touched on some part of his body, don't pet that place continuously, but come back to it often with a quick caress. This is quiet time, a time of pleasant communication through touch, not a battle of wills or a wrestling match, so don't push any issue. Keep your mind on the TV show and your strokes gentle and lazy, and soon Samson will be asleep. Now you can gently stroke the places he didn't want you to handle. Have you ever noticed that a new ring can be quite annoying, but after you wear it to bed it feels more natural? This is the same principle.

The World as a Playground

The world is Samson's big playground, and to enjoy investigating it, he should get out and around as soon as he is safely vaccinated. This part is the most fun. Few people can pass by a pretty puppy without wanting to touch it or talk to it, and that's what you're counting on, because your puppy needs these people. It needs to meet elderly folks and toddlers, gentle children and teenagers, young marrieds pushing strollers, bearded men, and women wearing big hats. While safely outside in your arms or on a leash, Samson will also become used to hearing motors, horns, sirens and the rumble of the garbage truck. The more people Sam meets and the more sights he sees, the more confident he will become, and this will make him a better companion and guardian all his life.

If your house doesn't have stairs, find some elsewhere and patiently teach Samson how to navigate them. To do this, put

The better socialized the puppy, the more activities it will enjoy as an adult. Sage-brush Tacoma Dreamer, TT, OFA, bred and owned by Carla Restivo, enjoys her pool and toys.

him on the third or fourth step, and encourage him to come down. When he becomes secure going down, sit on the third or fourth step and encourage him to climb to you. Soon navigating a flight of stairs will be a breeze.

Short car rides to the park, to visit a friend or even to nowhere are also important. Once or twice a week is usually often enough to get Sam used to the scenery and the motion. Soon he will relax and sleep peacefully in the car.

Of all the ways Samson needs to be socialized, one of the most important is also the most fun. Besides developing social skills around people, Sam needs the company of other puppies. In fact, the more puppies of all types he is able to play with, the more sociable and reliable he will become. Always use good judgment when choosing playmates and play groups. Puppies don't know their own strength (although playing with other puppies helps them learn it), so don't overwhelm your eight-week-old Pit Bull by putting it with a five-month-old Saint Bernard. And on the other hand, a tiny Toy Poodle puppy shouldn't have to endure the antics of a peppy, three-month-old Pit Bull, either.

Kindergarten Puppy Classes

Check your newspaper or the yellow pages in your phone book for kennel clubs or dog obedience schools, because some of them offer a helpful program called Kindergarten Puppy Training (KPT). Geared to young puppies, these classes introduce them to people, objects, situations and each other, while encouraging them to earn praise for a job well done and learn respect for the word "No." Not only are the classes fun for puppies and people, but they detect early signs of overaggression toward other dogs, so it can be corrected before it becomes a problem.

Noise Sensitivity

An occasional pup is especially sensitive to loud noises. This can be easily cured with patience and a bit of ingenuity. Simply think of every single thing Samson enjoys, then think of what kind of noise you can make to herald the fun. For example, if Sam looks forward to feeding time, stir his dinner in a metal pan using a metal spoon before giving it to him. Sometimes drop the pan (no closer than ten feet from him) before you fill it. If Sam looks forward to the children coming home from school, announce their arrival with applause and cheers. Tailor your noise-making to your own puppy's delights, and soon he will be happy and secure around loud noises.

Mad Dashes in Mindless Circles

Not just a trait of Pit Bull puppies, nearly all puppies suddenly run wildly around and around the room a couple of times a day, usually landing in their favorite position, tired but happy. Pit Bull puppies just happen to do it with amazing vigor. Why do they do it? No one knows. Will they ever stop? Maybe. Eventually some of them outgrow it.

Sudden Fear Syndrome

Somewhere between the ages of eight and eleven weeks, many previously happy-go-lucky puppies suddenly become leery of strangers, new places or objects. This is when it's especially important to remember the first rule of socialization. When Samson looks fearful, never reassure him by cajoling or petting, as he will interpret those actions as praise. Anything your puppy is praised for it will repeat again and again, and a hesitant, fearful stance could become its learned response to the sight of a new object. Never yank it toward a feared object, either. Treatment like that will turn a slight scare into full-blown terror.

Instead of feeding Sam's fear by babying him, or terrifying him by using force, just confidently approach the new object yourself. Touch it like it was long-lost treasure, and happily invite Sam over to see the wonderful thing. Sitting down by the feared object is an especially good way to encourage a puppy to move toward it. Summoning his baby bravery, Sam may crawl on his belly, nose outstretched, toward the feared object. After Sam has made his approach and examined the object, praise him for being a brave fellow. If the object is unbreakable and not too large, toss or roll it away from (never toward) him. This will arouse his natural chasing instinct, and before long he may be rolling and chasing the object himself.

Don't be surprised if the feared object is something as silly as a garbage bag or a fire hydrant. During the three or four weeks of the fear phase, Samson may see the bogeyman everywhere. Keep him away from loud noises such as guns or fireworks during that period, and steer clear of extremely crowded places. If you neither force him nor soothe him, the phase will pass, and sissy Sam will soon behave like sturdy Samson again.

CONDITIONING

Puppies between seven and sixteen weeks of age are too young for actual training but exactly the right age to learn how to learn. When you condition your pup to almost automatically give you the response you want, these good habits make later training much easier.

Come!—Carefree and Reliable

The most important response your dog will ever learn is to come when called. A reliable reaction to the come command keeps owners happy and saves dogs' lives.

Before Crystal can learn to come when called, she has to learn what "come" means. Decide how you want to call Crystal, then always use the same word or words. If you use "come" one time, "here girl" the next and "over here" or "let's go" after that, Crystal may come in response to all these commands if your tone is inviting enough, but she won't learn the meaning of the command.

After you decide how to call Crystal, use the command frequently. One of the reasons many grown dogs respond to the "sit" command more readily than they do to the "come" command is that their owners use the "sit" command much more often. Nowhere is the old saying "practice makes perfect" more true than in dog training. So look for excuses to call Crystal, and play calling games with her.

Bribery works best when teaching young Crystal what "come" means. Introduce the command "come" at feeding time by saying her name followed by "come" in a happy voice: "Crystal, come!" Show Crystal her dinner dish, and when she follows you and the dish a few steps, praise her and let her eat. Repeat this easy conditioning lesson every time you feed her.

Puppies love to chase, and you can use that instinct to your advantage. Always move away from Crystal when teaching her to come. When she is very young, call her only when you know she will want to come—not when she is eating dinner, playing with a toy or enjoying another person's company. Touch your puppy playfully, say "Crystal, come," and run away a few steps while bending, clapping and talking happily to encourage

Chaffy Isaac is proud she knows how to handle her grandmother's dog, Samson.

Crystal to reach you quickly. Let her catch you, play with her a few seconds, then call her and run off as before. Three or four times is enough. Always quit before Crystal wants to.

Your whole family can have fun with "come" games. Puppies love to find people, so games of hide-and-seek work great. Children can hide behind a chair or a door and call Crystal happily and often until she finds them. Then they should celebrate by petting and hugging her or giving her a little treat for being such a splendid detective. The more places the children hide, the better time Crystal will have, as long as the children are upbeat and patient.

Young puppies are insecure in strange places unless they are close to you, so take advantage of that to instill the "come" command. If possible, find a safe field, far away from traffic and other dogs, and allow Crystal to explore off lead. When she examines a flower, hide behind a tree. Then call her cheerfully. Praise her enthusiastically as she heads in your direction, and celebrate when she finds you.

Another conditioning trick that works well in a field is to suddenly turn and walk in a different direction when Crystal is investigating out ahead of you. After going a few steps, call her in a normal, happy tone (not excitedly, as you aren't hiding), and don't miss a beat in continuing to walk away from her. The slower she responds, the faster you should move away. When she arrives by your side, welcome her casually and continue walking. The next time she moves away from you, do it all over again.

Bold Belle, Slow Sue and Bashful Betty

There is no way your puppy can come and still be wrong, but some responses are more desirable than others. When you call Belle, if she comes bounding over eagerly with her tail wagging her whole body, hug her and tell yourself how lucky you are.

When you call Sue and she saunters slowly toward you, vary your actions upon her arrival. Sometimes hug and praise her. Other times, give her a treat. About half the time just give her a joyful pat, then turn and run away from her while calling her on the fly. Soon she will join in the fun by coming to you with more enthusiasm.

It's Bashful Betty, the puppy that lowers her body and creeps toward you that needs more help. She may become even more submissive when she reaches you, keeping her head down and possibly rolling over and presenting her belly.

Don't rub that cute belly to reassure Betty. Reassuring her is a mistake because it praises her submissive behavior. Instead, use the same happy talk you would use if she were an outgoing pup, but kneel down when she reaches you and cup her face in your hands. Tickle Betty under the chin. Get her to reach up for a treat. That encourages her to keep her head up and prevents her from lying down or rolling over. Don't despair over Betty's bashful behavior. Many actors and, yes, even politicians, were once shy children. When she outgrows her fear stage, Bashful Betty could become as bold as Belle.

Outdoors on a Leash

Wait until Crystal is used to walking on a leash before practicing the "come" command outdoors in a suburban or city neighborhood. Then, when Crystal is walking beside you nicely on a loose lead, call her and start walking or running backward.

Cheer Crystal on as she chases you, and reward her with play, praise, and sometimes a treat when you let her catch you.

Don't Cancel Your Conditioning

Suppose your neighbor invited you over for freshly baked brownies. Then, while you were happily munching, she steered the conversation to her allergies, wondering aloud if your new puppy was making them worse. After listening to her rehash her rashes, how would you respond to her next invitation?

After conditioning Crystal to come happily when called, don't erase your work by becoming lazy and calling her over so you can push a pill down her throat or chastise her for chewing your shoe. Always go to Crystal for the unpleasantries, and keep her "comes" carefree.

Leash-Breaking Your Puppy

When leash-breaking your puppy, a flat buckle collar made of leather or nylon works best. Leather stretches and puppies grow, so check the fit every few weeks. While the collar should not feel tight against your puppy's neck, it should not be loose enough to slide off over its head, either.

Chain training collars, also called choke chains, are useful when working with puppies five months of age or older. They are the collars most frequently used by people who compete in obedience competition. When purchasing a chain training collar, look for one that has small links and releases instantly. When tightened, it should have between $1^1/_2$ to $2^1/_2$ inches of excess chain before the ring attaches to the lead. The best-fitting ones are a little snug sliding over the dog's head. There is a right and a wrong way to put a choke chain on your dog. When worn correctly, the active ring (the one attached to the leash) will come across the *top* of the right side of your dog's neck.

For training Chief, you will need a leash that is six feet long and as wide as feels comfortable in your hand. For just plain walks, you might be more comfortable using a shorter leash.

Let Chief get used to the feel of a collar before starting to train. The first few times he wears one, play with him. If he is a chow hound, put the collar on just before feeding time. Let him wear it a little longer each session until he pays no attention to it.

When Chief is used to the collar, attach the lead and let him drag it around. Keep your eye on him so he doesn't catch it on something and start struggling. When he becomes nonchalant about dragging the lead (or if he did not drag it at all because he was too busy playing with it), take him to an open area, pick up your end of the lead and follow Chief wherever he takes you.

After Chief has enjoyed a few sessions of leading you, attach his lead to the doorknob of a door that will remain shut when he pulls, and let him fight it out with a solid object instead of you. Stay in the room, but ignore Chief for five minutes. If Chief protests passionately, one minute may seem like five, so remember to time it instead of guessing. Be prepared for Chief to scream and struggle, but if there is nothing he can get tangled in, he won't hurt himself. Working on this once or twice a day for a few days is usually enough. When screaming Chief becomes calm, and when he knows how to relieve the pressure on his collar, it's time to take him to an open area again.

This time allow Chief to lead you for a minute, then begin putting gentle pressure on the leash and choosing the direction you both go. Walk toward, not away from, familiar surroundings, and encourage him with happy talk. Chief doesn't have to be in any particular position—out in front, following behind or beside you are all okay at this point.

Gradually, as Chief accepts your leadership and becomes confident enough to walk both toward and away from home with you, reel him in a little closer if he tries to pull you. When he walks near you on a loose leash, occasionally lean down and play with him or praise and pet him. If he still persists in pulling, put the leash in your right hand and place that hand tightly against the front of your waist. Then put your left hand over your right to steady it. Pick a direction and start walking. Just as Chief is about to reach the end of the leash in front of you (an instant before he will pull), make a quarter-turn to the right and continue walking at the same pace. Do not warn him, call him or slow down for him, and wait until he catches up with you before talking to him. Then let him know you are delighted that he is by your side again by saying something like, "Oh, there you are," as you give him a quick, playful pat or a treat. Repeat when necessary.

Some puppies lag behind instead of pulling. If Chief is still way behind you after a few sessions, turn to face him and run backward while clapping and encouraging him with your voice. When he catches you, play with him. If Chief is very young, allow him to catch you when you see him make the effort.

Five minutes a day is enough when leash-breaking, and more than ten minutes is too much.

Obedience School

It would be ideal if every new Pit Bull owner enrolled his or her puppy in obedience school when the puppy was between five and seven months old. Veterinarians often know where such classes are held, or you can look them up in the yellow pages of your telephone book or in the classified ads section of your newspaper. For more on obedience classes, see chapter 9.

Of course, the ideal isn't always possible due to busy schedules and other considerations. If you can't attend classes, you can still walk with a mannerly Pit Bull if you do the following "sneakaway sessions" on your own schedule.

SNEAKAWAY SESSIONS

Pit Bulls, like all terriers, are ever alert to what is going on around them and want to investigate every new thing they see. This is a fine trait in a dog that is guarding your home, but it can make walking your dog a battle of wills instead of fun. Even if you are two hundred pounds of muscle, it's still no fun to have your dog lunging this way and that at the end of the leash instead of walking peacefully by your side. And even if you are ninety pounds of skin and bone, you can easily control your dog. How? First, stop talking. Then go the opposite of where your dog wants to go. Now you've begun sneakaway sessions.

Equipment and Use

Your puppy (or dog) should be wearing a snugly fitting buckle collar that it cannot back out of. In addition, make or buy a longe line—a fifteen-foot nylon line with a swivel snap at one end and a loop handle at the other. Put your right thumb in the handle of the line and clasp your fingers around the remainder of the strap. Then place your left hand under your right so there is no slack between your hands, and hold both hands in front of you against your waist. The full fifteen feet of line should be dragging on the ground.

Sneakaway sessions work on adult dogs as well as puppies. Just modify your speed to fit the size and age of your dog. Pit Bull puppies should be at least four months old before beginning sneakaway sessions. They should also be somewhat coordinated. If your puppy is still rather clumsy, walk more slowly than your normal pace.

Step One: A Little Respect

The first goal is to teach Ranger to walk within five feet of you on a slack line, in spite of distractions. Distractions are anything Ranger is interested in, such as cats, fire hydrants, birds, food, children, other dogs or the door to your house.

Imagine standing in the center of a large hula hoop with a five-foot radius. When Ranger steps outside this imaginary circle, silently and swiftly walk away from him, and keep walking until he comes back into a five-foot radius of you. If he passes you and continues out of your radius, turn and walk in the opposite direction. Ranger will be jerked when the line tightens because he isn't attentive enough to realize that you turned. Never move your arms to jerk him. The correction will be stronger and more meaningful when you keep your arms steady against your waist so that your full body weight powers into the line.

Even if you have an urge to warn Ranger before the line tightens, don't do it. To achieve the goal, your dog has to have his attention on you, not just one ear half-cocked in your direction. When Ranger can hear what you intend to do, he has no reason to watch you. Also, don't praise Ranger when he comes into your radius. Staying near you on walks is not something you should have to ask for and reward. Instead, it should become a way of life, an act of respect.

Why have Ranger on a slack fifteen-foot line when your goal is to keep him from pulling when he is on a regular four- to six-foot leash? Because holding him on a tight leash does nothing to teach him respect, attention and a sense of commitment to you. In fact, some Pit Bulls think a tight leash is fun and games, and the harder you pull, the harder they pull. The long, slack line allows you to build momentum so that the tug will be stronger if Ranger lunges away.

At first, the line may tangle in Ranger's legs. Usually he can easily step out of his mess if you continue walking slowly, but sometimes he may get hog-tied. When this happens, back up to put some slack in the line, take a step forward to tighten it and repeat until Ranger moves forward to loosen the line. Avoid returning to rescue him or he may learn to tangle himself for sympathy and attention.

Some Pit Bulls think the line is a wonderfully wiggly chew toy. Discourage Ranger from mouthing the line by having him wear it a few minutes a day in the house and commanding "No!" when he grabs it. If he won't drop it, spray Bitter Apple on the line.

Practice ten minutes a day for a week. With pups over six months old and grown dogs, you may speed results by training a half hour a day for two days before moving to part two. Don't rush. Grown dogs accustomed to pulling you down the street may need additional time to change their attitude.

Step Two: Dealing with Distractions

After Ranger consistently succeeds at staying in the five-foot radius, practice around distractions. They will teach him to ignore his impulses and remember his responsibilities. Use food dropped on the ground, animals and children, and practice in new places like parks, supermarket parking lots or near a kennel of barking dogs. When Ranger discovers that he can't focus on other things and watch your movements at the same time, he will become attentive to you.

Now, instead of walking, run away when Ranger leaves your radius, and stop dead when the line goes slack. When he is in your radius and attentive to you, walk slowly or stand still. If Ranger doesn't stop in your radius, turn and run in the opposite direction again. Running makes the correction stronger because you build more momentum. But don't try for track records when training puppies.

After several ten-minute, or a few thirty-minute sessions, combining tempting distractions with running away, Ranger should be watching your movements and staying close. If he lunges ahead, run straight in the opposite direction so he won't be able to see your actions peripherally. With a strong, adult Pit Bull that has a bad pulling habit, build the maximum momentum by running away fast instead of gradually building speed. If there isn't enough space in some areas for you to sneak away effectively, avoid taking your dog to those places until he is ready for part three.

Step Three: Real Life

Once you have Ranger's attention around a variety of exciting distractions and he seems to want to stay next to you on a slack line, you are ready to enforce the "no pulling" rule on a six-foot leash. Hold the loop with your right thumb and grab up the slack in your right hand. There should be no tension on the leash when he is standing beside you at your left side. Straighten your right arm with your knuckles against the right seam of your pants so the lead runs in front of your legs. Now walk briskly with Ranger on your left.

If Ranger tries to lunge ahead, open and close your hand so you drop the slack, thus giving him more rope. Grip the loop end, turn halfway around to the right and run as fast as you can until he is running behind you on a slack leash. Then fold the slack into your right hand again. If Ranger passes you as you run, turn and go the opposite direction until he is happy to stay near you. Don't jerk the lead at all. Your body will do that for you. If running is uncomfortable, walk with long, determined steps.

Ranger may try to walk directly behind you. Correct that by shortening the slack in the lead, and be sure your right knuckles are against the outside seam of your pant leg. Then walk straight ahead briskly, and the force of your left thigh thrusting into the leash with every step will bring him up beside you.

Now you have the know-how to teach your Pit Bull to take leisurely walks on a loose leash no matter who or what else is on the street, to stop rushing through gates and doors and to remain attentive to you even if another dog vies for its attention. Allowing Ranger to drag you around tells him that he is the leader mentally and physically, so be ready to sneak away anytime he forgets the "no pulling" rule.

From here on, your Pit Bull only has to learn to sit, down and stay on command, and his public behavior will be impressive.

ESSENTIAL EDUCATION

Every dog should respond to simple commands such as sit, down and stay. No matter what your Pit Bull's age, one of the following methods should help you take command.

Sitting Pretty

If your Pit Bull is younger than four months old, use treats to teach the sit. Puppies as young as seven weeks of age can be conditioned to sit, as long as the training is always upbeat and fun and the puppy is never yelled at or punished for forgetting the command.

Five-month-old Taylor has mastered the sit.

Little Lucy will love learning to sit on command if you begin by holding a small piece of a yummy treat in front of her nose. Say "sit," and move the treat over her head in such a way that her eyes follow it upward, her head tilts back and her rear reaches the floor. At that point, give her the goody. Practice this five or ten times, twice a day, and Lucy will soon know the meaning of the command "sit." A soft treat, such as a nibble of cheese, is the best teaching aid. It's healthy, and Lucy can eat it fast so you can continue training.

No matter how good a "sitter" Lucy becomes for treats, reinforce the command without showing her a goodie after she reaches four months of age. Place your right hand on Lucy's chest and cup her rear in your left hand. Say "sit" one time as if you mean it—short and firm, but not loud. Then push back slightly with your right hand and slide it upward to stop under Lucy's jawbone. Tickle gently under her chin to keep her head up. At the same time, push down and forward lightly on her rear. When Lucy sits, hold her in position for five or ten seconds using the least force necessary to get the job done. It's okay to give a goody after time is up, but don't do it every time, and don't let her see it until after she has remained in position for a few seconds.

Teaching Adult Pit Bulls to Sit

A more forceful method of teaching the sit works on puppies over five months of age that haven't responded well to the milder method. It also works on adult Pit Bulls. With Gus wearing a chain training collar and leash, place him beside you on your left. Take the active ring of the collar in your right hand, command "sit," and pull mostly up but slightly forward while your left hand pushes down and slightly forward on his rear. Relax the pressure on the chain the instant Gus sits. If he tries to move, tighten long enough to reposition him, then immediately relax the pressure again. You may have to kneel beside Gus to keep him in place for ten seconds.

Use only the amount of force necessary to get Gus to sit and remain in position for several seconds. Some dogs need only a slight pull on the chain and a light push on the rear. Others may need a quick, hard upward jerk on the chain while you practically sit on their rear. Praise quietly when Gus succeeds. Loud praise can easily excite an exuberant Pit Bull and make learning how to sit still extra difficult.

Teaching the Down

Teaching Rocky to down on command could be extremely easy, horrendously hard or anything in between, depending on his attitude. Some dogs can hardly stand being placed in a submissive position. Because dogs react in so many different ways, there are several methods of teaching the down. They are listed here from the mildest to the most forceful. It's best to try them in order, give each method a chance before moving on to the next one and stick with the mildest method that works.

Many dogs enjoy learning the down with treat training. Begin with Rocky in sit position, hold a tasty treat right in front of his nose and command "down." Think of making a movement shaped like a capital L as you lower the treat straight down just in front of his paws and then slowly pull it outward. As Rocky reaches for the goody, the front half of his body will move downward. If it doesn't lower completely to the ground, use your free hand to push lightly on his shoulders, but do not mash him down. The instant his whole body is in down position, give him the treat. If Rocky is younger than three months old, do not move on to any other method of teaching the down.

Puppies over three months old and adult dogs can try the "slide down." Start with Rocky sitting beside you on leash. Reach over him with your left hand and grasp his left leg at elbow level (high up on the leg). At the same time, take his right elbow in your right hand. Command "down," wait a second, then lift both his legs up just enough to slide them forward into the down position. If Rocky resists, lean on him with your chest while sliding his front legs. When he is down, praise quietly while keeping him steady for a few seconds. Then tell him "okay," and play happily with him as you allow him to get up.

Always remember to wait a second between giving the down command and starting the slide. Otherwise you won't realize it when Rocky has learned to go down on command. Practice about ten times a day until you can easily keep him in the down position for fifteen seconds.

If Rocky doesn't cooperate after a week of practicing the slide down, try the "jerk down." Use a chain training collar and sit him by your left side. Hold the leash in your right hand close to the snap and place your left index finger and thumb on either side of his spine just behind the top of his shoulders. Command "down," and pause a second so you will know if Rocky responds. If he doesn't respond quickly, snap the leash down sharply at an angle so that your hand ends up by his elbow. Your left hand pushes down at the same time. Practice until you can easily keep Rocky down for fifteen seconds, and praise happily when you give the "okay" signal allowing him to get up.

The Anxious and the Angry

An occasional dog hysterically resists downing. If yours has this problem, be certain to practice sneakaway sessions first. If it still refuses frantically, or shows any signs of anger whatsoever, please do yourself the favor of getting help from an experienced trainer.

Staying in Place

If your Pit Bull is over five months old and knows how to sit and down on command, it's time to make your life easier by teaching it to stay in place. Use a chain training collar and leash and begin by having Maggie either sit or down beside you. Then command "stay" and, at the same time, swing your arm just in front of her nose with your palm facing her. That's the stay signal. If Maggie moves from the sit, reposition (correct) her immediately using the forceful method of teaching the sit described earlier. If she moves from the down, reposition her using the jerk down. Don't repeat the stay command when correcting. The more you repeat commands, the more Maggie learns to ignore them. If she doesn't listen the first time, let your hand and leash do the talking through the forceful sit and the jerk down.

Begin with a goal of ten seconds, then slowly increase the time by five-second increments. Practice several times a day until Maggie will sit or down beside you for twenty seconds. Always pet and praise her when she achieves the goal.

Once Maggie stays steady on the sit and down with you beside her, step in front of her, still holding the leash. Now do a little play acting. Tie your shoe. Pull a weed. Examine a pebble. But have one eye on Maggie, and the instant she moves be ready to correct her. As Maggie improves, slowly work your way farther away from her but run in and reposition her instantly if she moves.

Remember distractions? You need them here. A dog that holds a stay only when it's bored won't make your life easier. You want Maggie to stay where she was told while your friend's toddler sucks on a spare rib. So practice stays on leash around other animals, children, friends and food, and continue to correct any movement immediately.

When Maggie does stays well on leash, replace her leash with a fifteen-foot longe line and begin increasing your distance from her by tying her to a post or tree. Now you can move farther away and use some new distractions. Just remember to return immediately to correct movement.

Eventually you will want Maggie to stay even though you are out of sight. To teach this, find a corner, such as the corner of your house. Place Maggie on one side, command "stay," and walk around the corner. Hold the longe line and toss out distractions such as treats or balls. Use a tiny mirror, or ask a friend to spy and to tell you what Maggie is doing. Then return quickly and silently to correct any movement. Practice in new locations with tempting distractions and soon Maggie will be so mannerly that your fussiest in-law will be impressed.

Earning an AKC Canine Good Citizen Certificate

The American Kennel Club has a program called the Canine Good Citizen Test, which is available to all dogs, whether AKC registered or not. Once your Pit Bull knows how to walk nicely on a leash and sit, down and stay in place, even with distractions, it should easily pass the ten-part test and earn a Canine Good Citizen certificate. Most Pit Bulls pass on their first try. To get all the details on this program, including a free copy of the test and training information, write to the American Kennel Club at 5580 Centerview Drive, Raleigh, NC 27606.

House Manners

Your dog may walk on leash like an obedience champion and obey commands well enough to impress Great-Aunt Bessie, but if it is a brat in the privacy of your home, it still isn't the pure pleasure it ought to be.

Your dog should understand and respect the word "No!" Use it when he's chewing something he shouldn't or getting into other trouble.

All dogs should learn to understand two words: "No!" and "Enough." "No!" means "Stop that immediately and don't ever do it again." Use of the word "No!" should be reserved for really bad behavior such as chewing the chair leg or nipping at feet or clothing. Your sharp tone and intense attitude when you bark out the word "No!" will not be lost on your dog. However, if it ignores you and continues chewing the chair, go to it and repeat your sharp "No!" while shaking it mildly by the scruff of its neck with a slight downward pressure. It will understand this, because it is similar to what its own mamma might have done to teach it the limits of her tolerance. Before long, it will respect the "No!" word.

"Enough" means "What you are doing is just fine sometimes, but you have been doing it too long (or too hard), so stop now." Use "Enough" when you don't want to throw the tennis ball anymore but your dog is still depositing it on your lap. Say "Enough" when the game of tug gets too rowdy, or when your dog continues barking long after the meter reader leaves. Said firmly, but without anger, "Enough" works on puppies, grown dogs and the children that are playing with them.

Housebreaking

Pit Bulls are basically clean creatures and do not want to soil their living, eating and sleeping area. When housebreaking, take advantage of this fact by confining Hogan to a small, safe area, such as a dog crate or one room of the house (an easily cleaned room, such as the kitchen or bathroom) every time you are away and he is left unsupervised. Then, as soon as you arrive home, take Hogan outside and praise him for doing the right thing. If Hogan soils his crate or his playroom, clean it up immediately. Besides being dangerous to his health, putting Hogan back into a wet or dirty crate teaches him to learn to live with his mess. That attitude will hinder, not help, the housebreaking process.

During this period of housebreaking, it is extremely important that Hogan be on a regular feeding and watering schedule. First thing in the morning, take him outside for several minutes and praise him for a job well done. When you bring him in, feed and water him and then take him outside again, as little puppies almost always relieve themselves immediately after eating. Confine Hogan when you leave the house, or even when you are at home but can't keep an eye on him.

At lunch time, take Hogan outdoors, feed and water him, and then take him outdoors again. Don't forget to confine him if you are leaving or are too busy to watch him.

When you arrive home in the evening, take Hogan outdoors and enjoy a nice long exercise period with him. Then let him watch you fix dinner or join you for the TV news. Feed and water him for the last time each day between 6pm and 7pm, then remove the water bowl until morning. Take Hogan outside when he finishes eating. After he relieves himself, enjoy his company for the evening. Take him outside again just before you confine him for the night and go to bed.

Sometimes Hogan will have to relieve himself more often than this schedule allows. When housebreaking, prevention usually works and correction usually doesn't, so watch him closely. When Hogan isn't confined, take him outside immediately if he begins walking in circles and sniffing the floor, or if he starts panting when he hasn't been exercising, or if he suddenly leaves the room. Also, most puppies have to relieve themselves after heavy exercise, so if you played hard on the rug, get Hogan off the rug and outdoors when play time is over.

All puppies make mistakes. If you get home too late and Hogan already had an accident, don't make a big deal over it. Your puppy won't understand what he did that made you so angry at him when he was so glad to see you, and that will lead to far worse problems. So, when the dirty deed was done before you got home, take Hogan outside anyway and he will eventually learn to expect the opportunity to go outside, and wait for it. Have patience and realize that Hogan may still be too young to control himself for the amount of time you were away. Clean up the soiled spot as soon as you can, using an odor neutralizer or plain white vinegar. Never use anything containing ammonia, as the odor of ammonia causes dogs to seek out the same spot to go potty again.

If you catch Hogan in the act, you may be able to stop him midsquat with a loud noise, like stamping your foot or clapping your hands. Then pick him up, hurry him outside to the right spot and praise him if he finishes what he started. Contrary to popular belief, spanking Hogan with a rolled up newspaper and rubbing his nose in his mess won't work. Punishments such as those teach a dog to eliminate in hiding, where he thinks you won't find it, not to go outside and do it proudly in front of you.

The keys to housebreaking are a regular routine and an alert trainer. A housebroken dog is simply a dog with a habit—the happy habit of eliminating outdoors.

Submissive Urination

Among animals in the wild, such as wolves, submissive urination means "You're the boss and I hope you're not angry at me, but if you are, I'm sorry." Dogs who greet their owners by submissively urinating (squatting and dribbling a few to several drops of urine while appearing happy but slightly shy), do not have a housebreaking problem. They have an anxiety problem that was caused either by heredity or by corrections that were too frequent or too harsh.

Never correct submissive urination, because that only makes it worse. To help Hogan overcome this problem, toss him a treat when you arrive home instead of talking to him, hugging him or leaning over him to pet him. Ignore Hogan until he comes to you for petting, then tickle his chest and under his chin instead of reaching over his head. Teach Hogan something easy, such as "sit," so you have reason to praise him. Praise builds confidence, and confidence is exactly what Hogan needs to conquer submissive urination.

Chewing

Between the ages of four to seven months of age, puppies have a real need to chew. This is because they are teething—gradually losing their milk or puppy teeth and replacing them with adult teeth. Your home and your personality will survive this stage if you give Hogan lots of toys made especially for chewing, such as rawhide sticks or bones, nylon or gummy bones, and rope toys. These are all available at any pet store and some supermarkets.

It is generally considered safe to let a puppy play with large nylon, gum or rope toys unsupervised, but rawhide toys can soften and get caught in Hogan's throat, so be in the same room with him when he is enjoying one of these.

One word of warning: Puppies don't know the difference between a worn-out shoe and your new leather boots, so don't give Hogan anything to teethe on except chew toys made especially for dogs. As soon as your puppy picks up something it shouldn't, simply go to it and take the item away. Then replace it with one of the puppy's own toys and praise it for chewing the right thing. After you do this enough times, Hogan will get the idea. In the meantime, confine the puppy when you can't watch it and be sure it has a safe toy to gnaw on in the confinement area.

The only time hitting your Pit Bull puppy is an acceptable training procedure is when it teethes hard on your hand or arm. If your "No!" doesn't stop it, tap it firmly (but not hard) under the chin. It's best if Hogan doesn't see the tap coming, or he may become hand-shy.

Jumping Up on People

Some people enjoy having their puppy joyfully jump on them the instant they come home. If you are one of those people, there is nothing wrong with that as long as you will still enjoy having Hogan jump on you when he is a forty- to sixty-pound adult. Because that's what will happen in a few short months.

The point is, don't allow baby Hogan to do something that you don't want him to do as an adult. In the case of jumping up, simply condition him to change his method of greeting people. Teach him to sit as explained earlier, then happily tell him to sit the instant you come in the door. When he does (whether you have to put him in position or not), meet him at his level and happily praise and pet him. Hogan jumps on you for instant attention, but if you withhold your affection until after he is sitting, then kneel down to pat and praise him, he'll soon understand what it takes to get approval and attention.

Possessive Over Food

Puppies compete with their brothers and sisters for food, and sometimes have to be deprogrammed when they enter a human family. Nothing to it. Just mix up these three choices, doing one during one meal and a different one later in the day, and after a week or so Hogan should understand that he no longer has to be possessive of his bowl.

1. Pet Hogan for a few seconds as he begins his dinner, then let him eat the rest of his meal alone.
2. Give Hogan only one-fourth of his dinner. Then, just as he finishes the tiny portion, put the rest of his meal in the bowl.
3. When Hogan is nearly finished eating, place a small but very special treat in his dish. A slice of hot dog, bit of

If noise becomes a problem, try one of the suggested remedies on page 133 for teaching your dog to be quiet.

hamburger or sliver of cheese will make him happy that you put your hand in his bowl.

If Hogan is still growly over his dinner dish after a week of alternating the choices above, use the strongest "No!" you can muster, complete with a scruff shake. If that doesn't calm him, seek help from a professional trainer.

Noise Stoppers

Most puppies bark and whine when their family confines them. Pit Bull puppies have the same reaction, but some of them make a sound resembling a blood-curdling scream. That's why you and your neighbors will be much happier if you condition Hogan during the daytime to accept confinement, instead of training him at night. There are several ways to squelch screaming, so begin with the least forceful and move ahead from there.

1. The first time you confine Hogan and leave him alone, try to put up with the noise for ten minutes without doing anything. Some puppies simply quit when they find themselves dramatizing to an empty theater.

2. A radio playing softly relaxes some puppies; in fact, they even seem to have musical preferences. But be sure to keep both the radio and the cord out of Hogan's reach.

3. If a little time and a radio don't help, make a sudden loud noise from another room such as stamping your foot or slapping the wall. Be sure not to say anything. It's best if Hogan thinks that his own racket, not you, caused the noise. As soon as he becomes noisy again, make the loud noise again. Repeat as often as necessary.

4. From the room next to the one Hogan is confined in, bang two metal pans together every time he barks, whines or screams.

5. Fill an inexpensive water pistol, not a high-powered one, and every time Hogan makes a racket, walk in silently and squirt him one time, directly in the face. Then walk out again. When Hogan is quiet for a couple of minutes, go to him without the water pistol and pet and praise him. Repeat as necessary.

With any of these methods, never take Hogan out of his place of confinement to stop his noise-making. That's exactly what he wants, so he will feel rewarded for complaining loudly. Wait until he is silent for at least a minute before going to him and letting him out.

Always be sure Hogan has a chew toy with him in his area of confinement. Nothing will keep him occupied longer than a sterilized bone stuffed with processed cheese (a long, rather thick, hollow bone that won't shatter, available at pet stores— you supply the cheese filling).

Puppies and people need a period of adjustment to live comfortably with each other. Always give Hogan enough attention so he feels loved and secure, and don't ever feel guilty about leaving him safely confined until he learns house manners. If you praise everything Hogan does right, and never reward fear or noise tantrums, you will raise a Pit Bull that you will enjoy and cherish all its life.

CHAPTER EIGHT

Caring for Your American Pit Bull Terrier

Hearty and robust, with a high tolerance for pain, your American Pit Bull Terrier should seldom show signs of sickness. In fact, if Cochise seems to be ill or in pain, it's a good idea to visit your veterinarian immediately. Pit Bulls prefer to appear brave and strong, and if Cochise can't keep up that pretense, chances are he is quite sick indeed.

When dealing with Pit Bulls, many of the most dangerous diseases are preventable through vaccinations, while other problems can be avoided through good nutrition, adequate housing, cleanliness, a bit of brushing and regular exercise. Next to you and your family, your veterinarian is Cochise's best friend. Take him to the vet for an examination within two days of bringing him home, whether his next vaccination is due or not.

VISITING THE VETERINARIAN

Feed Cochise lightly an hour or more before driving him to the veterinarian, as that may keep him from getting car sick. In any case, pack a roll of paper towels and a container of those wonderful wet wipes used on human babies. Bring along Cochise's health record and a stool sample in a small plastic bag. In the vet's office, keep Cochise on your lap or in his crate. Don't allow him to play on the floor or sniff strange dogs, as it's easy for young puppies to pick up germs.

Even if thinking about Cochise getting a shot makes you nervous, don't let him know that. Be friendly with the veterinarian, not nervous, or Cochise will feel your tension and become fearful himself. Hold Cochise in place gently for the veterinarian's examination, but as firmly as necessary. Talk to him in a happy, upbeat way, because if you console or coddle him, he'll be certain something terrible is going to happen. Cochise will take his cues from you. If he senses that you like the vet, he will like the vet, too.

VITAL VACCINATIONS, OR WHAT DO THOSE LETTERS MEAN?

When you bought Cochise, you should have received a list of his inoculations (shots) and his worming schedule, complete with the dates they were administered. Give this health record to your veterinarian so he or she can plan future treatments. The shots your veterinarian will schedule are the best preventative measure possible to keep Cochise from contacting a variety of potentially fatal diseases. The number and type of inoculations your veterinarian selects may depend upon your locale. If you plan to travel a lot with Cochise, tell your veterinarian, as exposure to strange dogs and new places may demand extra precautions. Don't take Cochise on any outings until you are sure that his inoculations are complete. Following his puppy series, Cochise will need a booster shot every year of his adult life.

KNOWING WHEN YOUR DOG NEEDS A VETERINARIAN

Your dog should be seen by the veterinarian if it shows one or more of these symptoms:

- A sudden inexplicable change in behavior
- An unusual discharge from any opening (mouth, penis, anus, vulva, ears, nose or eyes)
- Excessive thirst
- Frequent urination
- Straining during urination
- Blood in urine
- Straining when defecating
- Blood in stool
- Persistent diarrhea
- Persistent vomiting
- Persistent cough
- Lumps beneath the skin
- Loose teeth (in an adult), bleeding gums or horren dously bad breath
- Persitent lack of appetite
- Continuous weight loss
- Excessive hair loss or bald spots
- Peristent head shaking or pawing at ears
- Vacant, clouded or other abnormal look to the eyes

Signs of poisoning include:

- Watery eyes and either huge or tiny pupils
- Difficulty breathing or weak breathing
- Cold body
- Rapid heartbeat
- Staggering, twitching and extreme excitability
- Apparent pain
- Vomiting
- Excessive diarrhea
- Excessive slobbering
- Bloody diarrhea (not always evident)
- Paralysis of the rear end
- Coma

Combination shots have various names depending on the company that made them, but many of their names are made up of letters, such as DHLPP. This is what the letters stand for, and why those shots are so essential:

D Is for Distemper

Distemper is the number one killer of unvaccinated dogs and spreads rapidly from one dog to another. Its victims are usually puppies, although older dogs may contract it, too. Because distemper shows up in various forms, it is sometimes difficult for even experienced veterinarians to diagnose. While dogs with distemper occasionally recover, they often suffer permanent damage to their brain or nervous system. Symptoms of distemper include diarrhea, vomiting, reduced appetite, cough, nasal discharge, inflamed eyes, fever, exhaustion and lack of interest in toys or games. If you ever think your puppy has come down with distemper, take it to the veterinarian immediately. Dogs that receive treatment early have a better chance of survival.

H Is for Hepatitis

Infectious hepatitis in dogs is not transmissible to humans, although it affects the liver just as it does in the human form. In dogs, it spreads through contact with an infected dog's stool, urine or saliva. One specific symptom is intense thirst, but all the other symptoms are similar to those of distemper. The disease progresses rapidly and is often fatal, so prompt veterinary treatment is critical.

L Is for Leptospirosis

Leptospirosis (Lepto) is caused by a spirochete, a microorganism that is often carried by rats. It can infect a dog that has contact with a rat, or eats something contaminated by rats. Symptoms include bloody diarrhea or urine, fever, depression, red and congested eyes and mouth membranes, painful mouth ulcers, vomiting, increased thirst, loss of appetite, pain when moving, and the whites of the eyes may become red or jaundiced. The dog's kidneys and liver can be permanently damaged, so quick veterinary treatment is essential. Since humans can contact Lepto, it's important to carefully prevent infecting yourself when caring for a sick dog. Your veterinarian will explain the proper precautions.

P Is for Parvovirus

Parvovirus is a deadly killer that was unknown in dogs until 1977. It is believed to be a strain of feline distemper that mutated to infect dogs. The virus attacks the stomach lining, bone marrow and lymph nodes, and in young puppies, the heart. It spreads rapidly from dog to dog through contaminated stools, easily carried here and there via dog paws or shoes. Beginning with depression and a loss of appetite, symptoms soon progress to vomiting, diarrhea (sometimes bloody) and fever. Puppies with infected hearts (myocardial Parvovirus) often die suddenly or within one or two days of contracting the disease. Those few that recover may develop chronic heart problems later. How severely adult dogs are affected depends upon the individual dog. Some become violently ill, while others just lose their appetite for a day or two.

P Is Also for Parainfluenza

Parainfluenza has a couple of other names. Veterinarians may refer to it as infectious canine tracheobronchitis, while its common name is kennel cough. Highly contagious from dog to dog, Parainfluenza is caused by several different viruses, as well as a bacteria. Symptoms are a frequent dry, hacking cough and sometimes a nasal discharge. Other than that, the dog usually appears to feel fine, and many dogs infected with kennel cough don't even miss a meal. Dogs vaccinated against Parainfluenza sometimes come down with it anyway, but usually have milder symptoms than unvaccinated dogs. While the disease usually

To keep your Pit Bull in the best of health, like Spartan's Samson, CD, U-CD, U-CDX, TT, CGC, Ag. I, Ag. II, shown here playing flyball, take him to the veterinarian regularly. Samson is owned by Virginia Isaac.

runs its course, kennel cough is more dangerous to puppies than it is to adult dogs. They should be kept in a warm, humid room while recovering. For dogs of all ages, your veterinarian may prescribe antibiotics to prevent complications and medication to control coughing.

Rabies

Rabies is always fatal, and a dog with rabies is a danger to humans and other animals. The disease is a virus that can infect dogs that come in contact with squirrels, skunks, foxes, bats, cats, raccoons or other animals that already have the virus. It affects the nervous system, and is generally passed from animal to animal, or animal to humans, by infected saliva—usually from a bite. However, it may also infect a victim through cuts or scratches that come in contact with saliva from a rabid animal.

One of the first signs of rabies is a difference in disposition. A gentle dog may show signs of aggression, or an independent dog may suddenly crave affection. Soon the dog's pupils may become dilated, and light may appear to cause him pain. Eventually the dog will want no attention or petting at all, and may show signs of stomach trouble and a fever. Later symptoms can include lack of coordination, random biting, bared teeth, twitching facial muscles and loss of control of the facial muscles, resulting in an open mouth with the tongue hanging out. The dog's voice may change and it may drool, paw at its mouth and cough. Eventually it slips into a coma and dies. All warm-blooded animals are subject to the disease, so anyone bitten by a dog (or any other animal) should see a doctor right away.

Rabies vaccine prevents this dreaded disease. Your veterinarian will give the rabies shot separately, not in combination with the other vaccines. Some rabies shots are good for longer than a year, so ask your vet when your dog's shot should be renewed.

Prevention Pays

After that list of gloom and doom, how about a cheerful reminder? Preventative medicine can keep your beloved Pit Bull safe from all those deadly diseases. Just follow the vaccination schedule your veterinarian recommends.

WORM CONTROL

Besides vaccinating to prevent contagious diseases, your veterinarian should also check your dog for internal parasites, such as intestinal worms and heartworms. Your vet will need a sample of your dog's stool to check for roundworms, whipworms, tapeworms and hookworms, while a blood test is necessary to detect heartworms. No matter how carefully you care for your Pit Bull, it can still become infested with all of the worms except heartworm. Well-cared-for dogs shouldn't get heartworm, because their owners give them the preventative medication prescribed by their veterinarian.

The symptoms of roundworms, whipworms, tapeworms and hookworms are all similar, and include a rough, dry coat, dull eyes, a generally unsound appearance, weakness, weight loss despite an enormous appetite, coughing, vomiting, diarrhea and, sometimes, bloody stools. Few dogs have all of those symptoms and some dogs lose their appetite entirely when infested with worms. Other dogs show no symptoms at all until they become seriously anemic from a heavy infestation.

Don't be embarrassed if your Pit Bull gets worms. Many puppies are born with roundworms, and dogs can become infested with worms while out for a walk or from biting at a flea. Treatment is not dangerous and it is effective. The important thing is to have your veterinarian check your dog's stool at least twice a year; then give your dog the prescribed medication exactly as instructed.

Heartworms are a different story. They are transmitted from dog to dog by the bite of a mosquito, and eight months or more may go by from the time a dog is bitten until the worms mature. Treatment is dangerous (although less dangerous than the deadly worm), but your dog shouldn't have to undergo treatment because heartworms are preventable. Puppies can be put on preventative medication at a young age, and from then on should be tested annually. Because the medication may make a dog that is harboring adult heartworms critically ill, adult dogs must test free of the worms before they can begin a preventative regimen. Symptoms of heartworm infestation include a chronic cough, weight loss and exhaustion, as the worms interfere with the action of the dog's heart. Prevention is the only defense and it must be started early and continue throughout your Pit Bull's life.

EXTERNAL PARASITES

Fleas, ticks, ear mites and lice are all looking for a free lunch and a cozy home, compliments of your Pit Bull. Deer ticks are especially dangerous, as they may carry Lyme Disease, while other ticks may carry Rocky Mountain Spotted Fever. Never attempt to pull attached ticks off your dog by hand. Instead, use a preparation recommended by your veterinarian to safely remove them. Ear mites live in the ear canal, irritating your Pit Bull's sensitive ears and producing a dry, rusty-brown to black discharge. Lice seldom bother Pit Bulls, and when they do they are easily destroyed with modern preparations. Fleas, on the other hand, are never easy to get rid of. They quickly become resistant, or

GIVING YOUR PIT BULL A PILL

When your veterinarian prescribes pills that aren't the delicious chewable variety, the easiest way to give them is to hide them in a bit of cheese, peanut butter or some other soft treat with a strong odor. If your dog catches on to the deception and refuses the treat, or eats the treat but leaves the pill, you will have to resort to the following method.

- If you are right-handed, place your left hand on the dog's muzzle with your fingers pointing toward the nose, thumb on one side and fingers on the other.
- Squeeze inward and upward with your thumb and fingers. This will make your dog open its mouth and it won't want to close it because its lips are positioned between its teeth.
- Hold the pill in your right hand between thumb and index finger. Use your free fingers to push down on your dog's lower jaw and place the pill as far back on the top side of its tongue as you can get it with your index finger.
- Close your dog's mouth and hold it shut by keeping your left hand around its muzzle. Its nose should be pointing slightly upward. With your right hand, stroke your dog's throat (from behind the chin to the upper chest) and tell it what a good dog it is. Continue until you see or feel it swallow. Many dogs try to stick out their tongue immediately after they swallow, so that is a good clue that you have succeeded in medicating your dog.
- If you are left-handed, reverse the process.
- Never give a dog a pill unless it was prescribed or okayed by your veterinarian. Something as simple as an aspirin substitute (such as Tylenol, Motrin or Advil) can be harmful, and even fatal to dogs.

actually adapt to insecticides, so new flea dips, powders and sprays appear on the market every year.

For tips on how to discover if your Pit Bull has these pests, read the section on coat and skin care in the grooming section of this chapter. Have fleas already invaded your home? For an easy way to find out, read "Spring" in the section of this chapter subtitled "Adult Pit Bull Care for All Seasons." Your veterinarian knows which preparations work best in your locale, so if your dog or your home is bothered by creepy crawlies, ask for professional help. Your Pit Bull may never encounter any of the following problems, but it's sensible and safe to be aware of them.

Sarcoptic Mange

Sarcoptic mange is caused by mites. It will make Odie itch, and you will see tiny red bumps and patchy, crusty areas on his body, legs and/or stomach. Take Odie to the veterinarian. The condition is treatable and will respond to topical medication.

Follicular Mange

This mange is caused by a different type of mite. Also called demodectic mange or red mange, this condition may or may not make Odie itch. Whether it bothers him or not, you will notice small, circular, moth-eaten-appearing patches, usually on his head and along his back, sides and neck. Juvenile cases, involving a young dog with only a few patches, might be stress related. Perhaps Odie recently spent his first few days in a boarding kennel. Some females, for example, get a patch or two of mange when they come into season for the first time. Your veterinarian has medication to clear this condition, but if Odie ever gets a generalized case of this mange (covering much of his body), don't use him for breeding as he could pass the problem on to his young.

Ringworm

In spite of its name, ringworm is a fungal infection, not a worm. Carried more often by cats than dogs, ringworm causes small, round, itchy, bald patches, which are often inflamed because Odie can't help but scratch them. They are easily cured by the fungicide your veterinarian will recommend.

Just as these skin problems have similar symptoms, so do several others that Odie might encounter. Since it's difficult to determine exactly which condition is making Odie itch, and each one requires a different medication, leave diagnosis and treatment to your veterinarian.

CLOGGED ANAL GLANDS

If Odie is scooting along the floor on his haunches, he probably has clogged anal glands. His anal glands are located on each side of his anus and they secrete a substance that enables Odie to pass his stool. When clogged, they are extremely uncomfortable, smell bad and could become infected. Your veterinarian can quickly unclog Odie's anal glands, or you can do it yourself if you are game. Just use one hand to hold his tail up and, with a tissue or soft cloth in your other hand, take the skin on either side of the anus, just below the middle, in your thumb and forefinger. Then push in slightly and squeeze gently. If you succeed, a brownish, nasty smelling substance will be on your cloth and Odie will stop scooting. Blood or pus in the secretion is a sign of infection, so if either one is present, take Odie to the veterinarian.

HIP DYSPLASIA

Hip dysplasia is caused by an abnormality of one or both hip joints. If Odie has a borderline case, it may never be noticeable to him or to you, and the only way you would know is by having his hips X-rayed. In more severe cases, hip dysplasia causes lameness in the hindquarters, ranging in severity from a slightly odd gait to barely being able to stand. Hip dysplasia is incurable, but there are several ways to lessen its pain, including surgery in some cases. Your veterinarian will have to X-ray Odie to determine the best treatment for him.

All dogs, male or female, should be X-rayed and certified clear of hip dysplasia by the Orthopedic Foundation for Animals (OFA) before they are used for breeding. Your veterinarian will be able to guide you through the process.

Sagebrush Tacoma Danni, TT, OFA. "OFA" stands for Orthopedic Foundation for Animals, and means Danni's hips were X-rayed and certified clear of hip dysplasia.

RUPTURED CRUCIATE LIGAMENT

The cruciate ligament is in the stifle joint, and its rupture is similar to the knee injury that puts many top football players on the bench. This condition is an athletic injury that will cause Odie to limp noticeably or even refuse to walk on one rear leg. As this injury most often sidelines heavily muscled, extremely active dogs, the Pit Bull's structure and personality combine to make it one of dogdom's prime candidates for the problem. In most cases, a ruptured cruciate ligament must be corrected surgically.

DECIDING WHETHER TO CROP

The United Kennel Club Breed Standard for the American Pit Bull Terrier includes the following standard for ears: "Cropped or uncropped (not important)."

Ear cropping in the Bull and Terrier breeds had its origins in blood sports. Since ripped ears sometimes bleed profusely, some dogfighters cut the ears off their dogs so their opponents couldn't get an ear hold. Others left the ears natural, preferring the possibility of a torn ear over a leg, chest or throat hold. Today, ear cropping (sometimes called ear trimming) has no purpose but style, and cropped ears are shaped in an attractive prick-eared fashion.

Most Pit Bull breeders sell their puppies with natural (uncropped) ears, so shortly after you bring Ace home you will have to decide whether you want to have his ears cropped or not. In some countries, this decision doesn't have to be made. England, for example, outlawed cropping years ago, and Boxers, Schnauzers, Doberman Pinschers, Great Danes and other breeds that are almost always cropped in the United States retain natural ears there. Someday ear cropping may also be outlawed in the United States, but right now you still have a choice.

The best way to decide if you want to have Ace's ears cropped is to look at several cropped and several uncropped mature Pit Bulls and decide which style appeals to you. Many people feel that cropped dogs have a more alert appearance, while uncropped dogs have a softer expression and are more communicative with their ears.

Some veterinarians who have cropped other breeds may not have cropped an American Pit Bull Terrier. Consequently, you might make an appointment to have Ace cropped, only to have your veterinarian ask you to describe the proper style for the breed. If this happens, show your veterinarian the following sidebar, "Cropping the American Pit Bull Terrier." It was written by a veterinarian with much experience cropping American Pit Bull Terriers. There are several style variations, but the one described here is easy for a veterinarian who is inexperienced

You can choose to have your Pit Bull's ears cropped or uncropped. The dog on the left has natural ears, the one on the right has cropped ears.

CROPPING THE AMERICAN PIT BULL TERRIER

The correct APBT ear crop accentuates the massive head and muscular appearance of the breed. Since the cropped ear is relatively short, there is seldom any difficulty in getting the ear to stand after surgery. Because of the limited after-care, the age for cropping is not as critical as that of breeds where the ear style is much longer. Pit Bull puppies can be cropped at seven to eight weeks; however, waiting until twelve to fourteen weeks presents few problems.

Ear length is determined by laying the ear forward parallel to the eye without pulling or stretching. The cut is begun just short of where the medial edge of the ear meets the lateral canthus of the eye (see sketch). Proportionately, this is a bit shorter than a Miniature Schnauzer cut. The shape is distinctive to the American Pit Bull Terrier. There is no graceful curve to the ear as in the Boxer or Dobe. In fact, the ear edge is actually slightly convex from ear tip to base. The base is trimmed back cleanly to form a smooth, flat surface that blends into the cheek and neck.

Left: American Pit Bull Terrier. Right: Doberman Pinscher. (Diagram by Bonnie Wilcox, DVM)

A correctly cut ear on a pup looks just slightly longer than the ideal preferred ear. As the dog grows, the ears will become proportional to the head.

Ears that droop outward or hang after stitch removal can be trained to stand by rolling and taping the base. A week or two in tape is usually all that is required. Most American Pit Bull Terrier ears stand without any taping. Ear cartilage forming a crease at the head line can cause problem ears in some Pit Bulls. After surgery these ears tend to bend medially, often lying flat on top of the head. This is a difficult ear to train to stand correctly. A pup that has ears with this tendency should be cropped as early as possible, before the cartilage has begun to stiffen. This will allow maximum time for training and taping the ears into the proper position.

—Bonnie Wilcox, D.V.M.

with Pit Bulls to successfully perform. In fact, hundreds of dogs with successful show careers have sported this style.

NUTRITION

Good nutrition is essential to prevent dietary deficiency diseases. It also helps ward off infections and reduces your Pit Bull's susceptibility to organic diseases.

Bargain dog food is seldom a bargain. Even though the nutritional information on the package says it has the same amount of protein as the better-known brands, what's important is the amount of usable (digestible) protein. For example, shoe leather is protein, but it has no nutritive value at all. There is a fine selection of dog foods available for all stages of Teddy's life. Choose a reputable brand of puppy food, one that has been on the market for many years, then feed Teddy according to label directions and he should be well nourished. If you change brands from what his breeder fed, mix the new brand with the old, increasing the amount of the new brand gradually until the changeover is complete. Make the change in the same gradual way when Teddy reaches a year old and is ready for adult dog food.

While Teddy is growing, remember to gradually increase the size of his meals as he gets bigger. At seven weeks old he will need to eat three meals a day. By the time he is five months old, he will probably need about twice what he ate when he was

USING COMMERCIAL DOG FOOD

Most commercially prepared dog foods are balanced to provide your dog with optimal nutrition and are far healthier than anything you could create at home for twice the price. The proper balance of vitamins and minerals, fats and proteins is too complicated to guess at and is better left to the test kitchens of the major food companies. Another danger is our human tendency to think if some substance is good for bones or appetite, then a lot more will be even better. This is definitely not true and, in some cases, more is actually toxic.

Commercial dog foods fall into three major categories: canned, dried and semimoist. When planning to use only canned food, it is important to read the label carefully. Some canned foods provide total nutrition while others are formulated to be mixed with dry food. If the canned food is meant to be fed alone it will say something like "100 percent complete," or "complete dinner" on the label. Some canned dinners are available either "chopped" or "chunky." The nutritional values are equal, but most puppies find it easier to eat the chopped variety, while adult Pit Bulls often prefer their food chunky.

Dry dog foods come in a variety of shapes and sizes. Some types are in meal form, with the ingredients simply mixed together. Biscuit food may be made up of whole biscuits or crumbled biscuits. It is formed by adding flour to the dry ingredients and baking the

Whatever you feed your dog should leave her looking good and feeling good, like Starfire, shown here winning her Grand Championship.

mixture. Some dog foods are pelleted. This is actual meal-type food pressed into pellets. Read the labels on the dry food you buy because some are meant to be fed dry, others form gravy when moistened and are meant to be fed slightly wet and some may be fed dry or moistened. Many Pit Bulls do well on two-thirds dry and one-third canned foods mixed together.

While convenient and less expensive than the better-quality canned foods, semimoist foods usually have a high content of salt, sugar and preservatives.

There is no reason to change dog foods after you find a high-quality one that your Pit Bull enjoys, provided it feels well and looks good after six months of eating it.

Dog foods have eye appeal to attract you, not your dog. Dogs won't get bored with the same food every day like people would, and don't need to discover new shapes, colors and sizes in their bowls at frequent intervals. As long as you are feeding a recognized, high-quality food and your dog is thriving, it is unlikely that any change would be for the better.

There are special times in a dog's life when supplementation may be advisable. Females that have been bred and nursing females may need a little extra, especially if their appetites are suffering. Show dogs may be stressed from constant traveling and competing. If you think your American Pit Bull Terrier might benefit from supplementaiton, check with your veterinarian. He may suggest the addition of cottage cheese, hard-boiled (never raw) eggs, raw beef or liver, or a little fat to your dog's diet, or may put it on a prepared vitamin-mineral powder or tablet.

three months old, but he doesn't have to eat as often. By then, two meals a day are sufficient. As an adult (over twelve months old), Teddy will probably eat slightly less than he did as a growing puppy and will only need to eat once a day. Look at him to tell whether or not his food keeps him in top condition. Teddy's coat should shine, his eyes should be bright and he should be in good, solid flesh. Whatever you do, don't allow Teddy to become fat. Roly-poly puppies may look cute, but many serious health problems in dogs have been traced directly to obesity.

During adolescence (five to eleven months or more of age), Teddy may appear rangy and gangly, but as long as he has boundless energy and a gleaming coat, his nutritive requirements are probably being met. Poor nutrition almost always

WHAT DOES WHAT IN YOUR DOG'S FOOD

All dogs require food containing the proper proportions of carbohydrates, proteins, fats, vitamins and minerals.

Carbohydrates aid digestion and elimination, provide energy and the proper assimilation of fats. Excess carbohydrates are stored in the body for future use.

Protein is not stored, so your Pit Bull must receive it every day of its life. It is used for bone growth, tissue healing and the daily replacement of body tissues burned up by normal activity.

Fats are necessary as an energy source and to add shine to your dog's coat and suppleness to its skin. But excess fats are stored under the skin and can result in an overweight dog. Fat balance is important. Too much leads to the same obesity that humans suffer, while too little will not provide your Pit Bull with any protection from changes in temperature, and can result in a dog that is overly sensitive to cold.

Vitamins

- Vitamin A is necessary for a healthy, shiny coat because it is used by the dog's body for fat absorption. It is also essential for normal growth rate, good eyesight and reproduction.
- The B vitamins protect the nervous system and are also mandatory for normal coat, skin, appetite, growth and eyes.
- Dogs synthesize Vitamin C in their liver so it isn't often mentioned in an analysis of commercial dog food or vitamin preparations. Some breeders add it anyway, believing that it aids healing in the event of injury, helps to prevent hip dysplasia and fights bacterial infections.
- Healthy bones, teeth and muscle tone are all dependent on Vitamin D, but the vitamin must be taken in the correct ratio with calcium and phosphorus.
- Vitamin E is associated with the proper functioning of the muscles and the internal and reproductive organs.
- Most dogs are able to synthesize Vitamin K in their digestive tract, and this vitamin is essential to normal clotting of blood. If your dog seems to bleed too much and too long from a minor cut, mention it to your veterinarian. It could indicate a lack of Vitamin K.

- Calcium and phosphorus must be present and in the correct ratio to provide puppies with protection from rickets, bowed legs and other bone deformities. They aid in muscle development and maintenance, as well as lactation in nursing bitches.
- Potassium is needed for normal growth and healthy nerves and muscles.
- Sodium and chlorine help your Pit Bull's appetite and allow it to enjoy a normal activity level.
- Magnesium is necessary to prevent convulsions and problems with the nervous system.
- Iron is needed for healthy blood that prevents fatigue from anemia.
- Iodine prevents goiter in dogs as it does in humans.
- Copper is necessary for growing and maintaining strong bones and, like iron, helps to prevent anemia.
- Cobalt aids normal growth and keeps the reproductive tract healthy.
- Manganese also aids growth and is used in reproduction.
- Zinc is involved in normal growth and is also an aid to healthy skin.

shows up first in the quality of the coat. If Teddy's coat is dry or dull, consider it an early warning signal that something is wrong. Have your veterinarian examine Teddy, as it's possible that the quality and quantity of his food are fine, but he might need to be wormed or treated for a condition unrelated to nutrition. If his nutritional needs are not being met, your veterinarian may recommend that you change brands of dog food. This must be done gradually, and it will be several weeks before you will see a difference.

Some owners like to supplement their dog's diet with vitamins. Over-supplementation is dangerous and has been linked to a variety of ills, including hip dysplasia, so if you want Teddy to take vitamins, give them according to your veterinarian's directions.

Many adult dogs retain their proper weight consistently when fed a little extra during the winter and a little less during the heat of summer. Teddy may show less interest in his food during the warm months and turn into a chow hound by November.

When Teddy grows old, he may show less interest in his food for a number of reasons. One of them is sore teeth. If dental problems are causing Teddy pain, your veterinarian can make feeding time a pleasure again. If age is dulling Teddy's senses, warming his food will give it a more appetizing aroma. Also, offering much smaller amounts of food several times a day, instead of one big dinner, sometimes entices an old dog to eat.

EASILY AVOIDED ERRORS

- Don't feed your Pit Bull chocolate or any highly spiced or greasy, salty foods. Chocolate is deadly to some dogs, and spicy sauces and junk food lead to stomach upsets.
- Don't believe ads that encourage you to vary your dog's diet. Dogs do best when they are fed the same brand of food daily at a regular hour. If you must add something to your Pit Bull's food dish, mix a few tablespoons of a high-quality canned dog food with his dry dinner.
- Don't fill your puppy with table scraps. Puppies can't hold much food at a time, and no matter how nutritious your dinner is for humans, chances are its puppy food is better for it. Also, dogs that eat table scraps often lose their taste for dog food completely.
- Don't give your Pit Bull any bones other than cooked knuckle bones. Chicken, turkey or pork chop bones, for example, can shatter and slice open its intestines with their sharp points.
- Don't leave your Pit Bull's food dish down for longer than ten minutes. If it hasn't finished its food by then, remove it until the next feeding. That helps your dog learn to eat when and what it is fed.

CLEANING CHORES

Teddy's food and water dishes must be kept clean to prevent the growth of disease-producing bacteria and other dangerous microorganisms. Also, his play area should be frequently picked up with a poop scoop, as this will help control worms and biting insects.

EXERCISE

The muscles rippling beneath Frankie's sleek coat are not the only muscles that are toned and strengthened by regular exercise. Her heart and uterus are almost entirely made up of muscle, and even her intestine contains muscle tissue. The supply of blood circulating through these muscles is dependent on regular exercise. If Frankie leads an active life she will live longer, look healthier, behave better and whelp (have puppies) easier.

There are many ways to give Frankie exercise. Brisk walks are wonderful and are good for both of you. If you don't want to walk every day, teach Frankie to play ball or Frisbee and you can exercise her while sitting or standing in place. Give her a securely fenced play area, with a couple of dog toys and an old car tire, and she will exercise herself. Many Pit Bulls love to play with tires, and get sufficient exercise by lugging them around and play-wrestling with them.

Other excellent exercise includes getting Frankie ready for competition in obedience, weight pulling or agility. The form Frankie's exercise takes isn't important, but it is important that she get regular exercise in some form all her life. When she is young, she will help you discover games that will exercise her. When she is old, Frankie will still require regular exercise, but it may be up to you to initiate it.

GROOMING

There are few jobs more difficult than trimming the nails of a mature, fifty-pound Pit Bull that isn't accustomed to having her feet touched. But if you condition Angel from puppyhood to accept grooming as a regular part of life, she will soon learn that being handled and brushed is both pleasant and serious. Pleasant

Kim Herron rests with Spartagus after playing Frisbee. Photo by Cindy Long.

because it feels so good. Serious because she is expected to behave. If Angel becomes fidgety about being handled on any part of her body, tell her "No" sharply and firmly. By the time she is half grown, she should be steady and cooperative when you groom her.

Coat and Skin Care

Just a few minutes of daily brushing with a horse hair glove (or any brush with soft to medium bristles) will keep Angel's skin and coat healthy and shiny. Brushing stimulates circulation and the secretion of natural skin oils while it removes dirt, dead hair, loose skin particles and dandruff. If Angel's dandruff becomes a problem, moisten a cloth in Listerine mouthwash and rub it through her coat.

While brushing, check for ticks. Although easy to spot on a Pit Bull's sleek coat, sometimes they hide in the ears, between the toes, in the slightly thicker hair of the neck or in the rump area just before the tail. To uncover fleas, rough Angel's coat the opposite direction from the way it grows. You may not see any of the little pests move, but tiny black specks on the skin are a sign that fleas are there. Purchase insecticide shampoos and dips on your veterinarian's recommendation, and always use them exactly as recommended on the label.

Teeth and Toenails

To check Angel's teeth for tartar, hold her head firmly and lift her lips upward. A soft toothbrush or damp washcloth dipped in baking soda usually removes discoloration on the teeth. If the stains are not easily removed, ask your veterinarian if Angel's teeth need a professional cleaning. Hard dog biscuits and nylon chew toys will help keep a young dog's teeth white, but aren't enough to do the whole job.

Angel's toenails are too long if they make clicking noises on the floor when she walks or touch the ground when she is standing still. Dogs with very long nails tend to walk on the back of their feet, leading to splayed toes and an unattractive gait. Not only is this uncomfortable for the dog, but there is an additional danger. If untrimmed, toenails and dewclaws eventually curl under the foot, circling back to puncture the pads. This problem doesn't occur in wolves, coyotes or even stray dogs, because in their quest for food, they cover enough ground to wear their toenails down to a practical length.

To clip Angel's nails, lift her foot up and forward. Then hold it securely in your left hand so your right hand can do the trimming (reverse this if you are left-handed). If Angel has white nails, your job is easier than if her nails are dark. There is a blood vessel called the quick in the bottom stem of the nail that is clearly seen through white nails. Trim the nail just outside the quick. You won't be able to see the quick in dark nails, so make the cut just outside the hooklike projection on the underside of the nail.

When you cut the nail properly, Angel will feel nothing more than slight pressure, the same as you feel when cutting your own toenails. If you accidentally cut the quick, Angel's nail will hurt and bleed. Stop the bleeding with a styptic pencil made for human use, or use the styptic powder sold at pet supply stores.

Pressing the bleeding nail into a soft bar of soap for a minute or so will also stop the bleeding. Try to work under good lighting so you can cut Angel's nails without a mishap. Angel will forgive a cut quick if it is a rare occurrence; but if you are clumsy too often, she may begin to resist work on her feet.

Bathing

Since brushing cleans the coat and reduces body odors, Angel will rarely need a bath if she gets three to five minutes of brushing daily. Bathe her only when necessary, because shampooing dries the coat by washing away natural oils.

Equipment for a bath includes: old clothes (when Angel shakes, you'll be as wet as she is); a tub, preferably with a drain so Angel won't be standing in soapy water; a rubber mat for traction in the tub; a spray-nozzle hose attachment or a pail for dipping water; pH-balanced dog shampoo or insecticide shampoo (and a flea and tick dip if necessary); cotton balls; a washcloth; mineral oil; and a large towel or two. Coat conditioner following the shampoo is optional.

Before bathing Angel, allow her to exercise outside for a few minutes. That way she won't have to dash outdoors to go potty (and probably roll in the loose garden dirt) immediately following her bath.

Angel's bath water should be warm but not hot. Begin by placing a cotton ball inside each of her ears, to keep the water out. Next, spray or pour water over Angel's whole body with the exception of her face and head. Put a small amount of shampoo on her back and massage the lather well into her coat. Then add more shampoo as needed to clean her legs, neck, tail and underbelly. If you accidentally get soap in Angel's eyes, put a few drops of mineral oil in the inner corner of each eye to relieve the sting. Use the hose or pail to thoroughly rinse off the lather. Don't rush this step. Shampoo left to dry in the coat makes it dull and can cause intense itching. If you are using insecticide shampoo or dip, follow the label directions carefully.

Finish by wiping Angel's face and head with a warm, well-wrung washcloth. Remove the cotton from her ears and wipe them out with a dry cotton ball dipped in a bit of mineral oil. Then wrap Angel in a towel, lift her from the tub and towel-dry her well, especially her chest and underbelly.

ADULT PIT BULL CARE FOR ALL SEASONS

Each season brings its own beauty and its own brand of fun for you and your Pit Bull, from sniffing dewy dandelions to playfully pawing new snow. But changes in temperature, and even holiday celebrations, can have a dangerous side too, so take a few precautions and help Scout safely enjoy his whole year.

Spring

Along with the showers and flowers come pests. Of these, the mosquito, carrier of heartworm larvae, is potentially the most dangerous. Since mosquitoes are most abundant between April and October (except in the Deep South where there is no respite from their bite), every dog should be tested in the early spring. If Scout tests free of heartworm, your veterinarian will start him on another season of preventative medication. *Never give the preventative without having Scout tested first.* The medication can be fatal to a heartworm-infected dog, so if Scout tests positive, he will need immediate treatment to get rid of the parasites before beginning a preventative program.

Since you will be visiting your veterinarian anyway, spring is an appropriate time to update Scout's booster and rabies shots. The so-called "permanent shot" Scout received following his series of puppy shots is only permanent in the sense that he no longer needs frequent puppy shots. But he still must have a booster shot once a year. (Twice a year may be safer in some parts of the country, but that is up to your veterinarian.) Don't forget to bring along a stool sample for the fecal exam. That one determines if Scout is harboring any worms in his body tissue or intestines.

If fleas are a problem in your area, ask your veterinarian's advice on prevention or treatment, because some dogs are dangerously sensitive to flea products. Dogs react to fleas in various ways. A dog that is allergic to flea bites may become miserable over one or two fleas, while another dog may be quite infested without giving any indication. Your veterinarian can treat the allergies, but unless you get rid of the fleas, Scout will itch again in no time.

With flea prevention, earlier is better. Fleas are capable of producing another generation every twenty-one days, and one female can produce thousands of eggs in her lifetime. Once Scout is infested, your house may be, too. One way to check for fleas in your house is to take a large, shallow pan, fill it with water and add some liquid dish soap. Before retiring for the night, put the pan on the floor and place a desk-style lamp next to it with the light aimed at the water. After you go to bed and the lamp is the only light in the house, fleas will jump at it, fall in the water and sink immediately, because the dish soap made the water soft. In the morning you will know if there are fleas in your home or not. If you are not in a hurry, you may choose to use this water-and-lamp method to control the fleas in your home. The "bombs" sold in pet supply stores, supermarkets and veterinary clinics are faster, but check with your veterinarian before using them. Always read and carefully follow the directions on all fleas and tick products.

Beware of red ants (fire ants) in any place where Scout plays. You can't put poison in your dog's yard, so try pouring boiling water on the nest several times. Be careful where you stand while pouring, because ants near the nest could bite your feet. Another method is to use a poop scoop or a shovel and take a bunch of ants from each nest and place them on the other nest. Maybe they hate each other as much as we detest them, because for some reason that makes them leave. Once your yard has been infested by red ants, check it frequently. Long after you think they are gone, they often reappear in a different place.

Dangerous chemicals that commonly appear in springtime include the pesticides and herbicides used in gardening, radiator coolant (which tastes wonderful to dogs and cats but kills them), swimming pool conditioners and even suntan lotion (not meant to be swallowed, so don't let Scout lick you when you have it on). Everything is blooming in the spring and some attractive plants are exceedingly poisonous when chewed or eaten. If Scout is a vacuum cleaner on legs, it's a good idea to keep the number of your local or state poison control center in a handy place where you can find it even in a panic.

When caring for your dog's spring coat, a daily brushing and a bath should help remove loose, dead hair. Are you proud of Scout's glossy black brindle coat? If you want it to stay that way, let him play outside for extended periods only during the early morning and late afternoon and evening hours. Otherwise the sun will change his coat color to rust and its texture to dry.

If Scout is outside during the evening, an electric bug zapper in the yard is desirable. It will get most of the bugs, but not the flies. If you use fly bait, be extremely careful because it can be fatal to Scout if he eats it.

Summer

Scout must always have fresh, clean water available, especially if he is outdoors—and just because you filled his dish first thing in the morning doesn't mean he still has water while you are at

If your dog is kept outside during the summer, make sure he has access to lots of shade and fresh water.

SUMMERTIME HAZARDS

Heatstroke

A dog suffering from heatstroke must have immediate attention. Sometimes only a cold water enema, applied by a veterinarian, will save it. Symptoms include some, but usually not all, of the following:

- Rapid or heavy breathing with the mouth and tongue a very bright red
- Thick saliva
- Vomiting
- Bloody diarrhea
- Unsteadiness on its feet, and possibly falling
- A hot, dry nose with legs and ears hot to the touch
- In extreme cases the dog may be glassy-eyed and its lips may appear gray

When a dog's rectal temperature is 104 degrees or more, it is in serious trouble. If you suspect heatstroke, immediately take your dog somewhere cooler, and wet it down gradually with cool (not ice cold) water. Give it cool water to drink, but in small amounts at a time, never all at once. Apply cold compresses to its belly and groin area, but do not suddenly place an overheated dog in extremely cold water. While cooling your dog, make preparations to get it to the veterinarian.

Be especially cautious if your dog has already suffered a heatstroke and survived. After a dog has one such stroke, it seems to be more prone to getting another.

Snakebite

Symptoms of snakebite include swelling, labored breathing, glazed eyes and drooling. The best first aid you can give while rushing your dog to the veterinarian is to keep it warm, and as calm and inactive as possible.

Lyme Disease

Caused by the deer tick, symptoms include fatigue, loss of appetite, fever and sometimes swollen glands in the neck. In areas where the deer tick is prevalent, avoid those wonderful walks in the woods, keep your own lawn well trimmed and take precautions to keep field mice from nesting in your home. When you visit your veterinarian, ask for preventative suggestions based on your area of the country.

work. Some Pit Bulls consider everything around them a toy and will overturn their water dishes or play in their buckets. If Scout regularly upsets weighted water dishes, attach a galvanized steel bucket to the fence or to the side of his dog house. Should he figure out how to tip that, go to a feed and horse supply store and purchase the type of bucket-holder used in stables.

If Scout is lethargic, depressed or lacks appetite after upsetting his water, he may be in danger. To check, pinch up a fold of skin from his back and release it. If it does not flatten back into place immediately, Scout is dehydrated. This is an extremely serious condition that requires prompt medical attention. Your veterinarian may have to administer fluids subcutaneously (under the skin) or intravenously (into the vein).

When Scout must be outside in the summer, be certain that shade is present in part of his exercise area at all times. Remember that the section of yard that was shady when you put Scout out in the morning could be sizzling under the afternoon sun while you are away. Natural shade from trees and shrubs is best because regular evaporation of moisture from the leaves cools the air, but be careful not to plant anything that is poisonous when chewed. When erecting a shelter, use shade screen over the top and down a side or two. If it isn't placed in a shady, sheltered area, a doghouse alone can become dangerously hot when the sun beats down on it. And if you don't provide Scout with a shady spot, he may be forced to dig a cool ditch in your flower garden to bed down in.

If Scout spends most of his time in your air-conditioned home, don't put him out in the heat of the day for prolonged

TRAVELING: WITH OR WITHOUT YOUR PIT BULL

When vacationing with your dog, remember to pack easy, efficient clean-up items, like a poop scoop or heavy plastic baggies. It's important that you clean up after your Pit Bull. Each year more and more hotels and motels refuse to accommodate dogs because of the dirt and destruction left behind by a few irresponsible owners.

Because strange water causes diarrhea in some dogs, it's smart to carry water from home or buy bottled water along the way. Also bring dog food from home, portion-packed for easy use. Sometimes it's difficult to find your dog's brand on the road, and a sudden switch to a different food could cause an upset stomach.

When driving with the air-conditioner on and crated dogs in the back of a station wagon or van, check occasionally to make certain the air is reaching them.

Never take anything for granted, especially equipment. A modern motorhome recently became a death trap for several show dogs. The owner was watching the show and thought her dogs were comfortable inside her air-conditioned vehicle. No one realized that the air-conditioner had quit, because the generator was still humming along. Six dogs died.

Take care not to overexercise your dog when the humidity is high. The day will feel hotter than it actually is, and your Pit Bull may breathe noisily or appear to have difficulty breathing. Carry ice, water and towels on even short trips because you may get into a traffic jam or have a flat tire. Your dog can stay cool by licking ice cubes and lying on a wet towel, even if you are stuck on the side of the road for hours and unable to run your air conditioner.

Be wary of undertows (strong currents) when allowing your Pit Bull to swim in rivers and in the ocean. After your dog swims in salt water or chlorine, wash it with fresh water. Doggie life preservers are available in all sizes and are excellent for fishermen and boaters who take their Pit Bulls out to sea with them. It is extremely difficult to rescue a dog that has fallen from a boat in heavy seas, and even a top swimming breed can eventually become exhausted and drown. A life vest will help your Pit Bull maintain buoyancy, and the convenient handle will make water rescue easier.

Vacationing without your Pit Bull may require putting him in a boarding kennel. Plan ahead so you can get references from friends, and tour the facility before deciding to leave your dog there. Ask what medical records you will need to bring along, and beware of any boarding kennel that doesn't demand that your dog be up to date with his inoculations. Also, find out what brand of dog food the boarding kennel uses, and buy some about a week before leaving. Then get your dog used to the brand by mixing it with its regular food, adding a little more each day. If your dog dislikes it, or if it changes its stool, ask if you may bring premeasured servings of your Pit Bull's regular dinner.

periods. Give him most of his outdoor exercise in the early morning and evening, with just a quick trip to the yard to relieve himself, if necessary, at midday. No matter where Scout spends most of his time, avoid strenuous play or exercise during extreme heat.

Don't overfeed Scout in the summer. Obese dogs suffer from the heat more than dogs of normal weight, and dogs need fewer calories during the summer than they do the rest of the year. Also, try to schedule Scout's feeding for the cooler part of the day.

To keep Scout's sleek summer coat beautiful, brush it regularly. It stimulates the skin and promotes air circulation.

Pit Bulls can sunburn and suffer blistered ears and noses just like people. Does Scout have a light coat and pinkish skin? If so, be especially careful. Shade, not suntan lotion, is the answer, because Scout may lick the lotion from his nose and become quite ill.

When crating Scout during the summer, a strong wire crate is best because wire crates have ventilation all the way around. Heat can build up inside a plastic airline crate. Be certain Scout's crate is in a cool shady spot and there is water available.

Extreme heat kills sperm, so when Scout rests on a hot surface he may become temporarily sterile. If he is used at stud during the summer, the breeding should take place during the coolest part of the day, or indoors, in air-conditioning.

On the Fourth of July, keep Scout indoors and safely confined. Some dogs become so frightened by the noise and flashes of light that they break loose and run away—usually into the street. If fireworks scare Scout, celebrate another way or away from home. Be sure to confine Scout before you leave, so your neighbor's fireworks won't frighten him.

The temperature inside a car or truck, even one parked in the shade, is usually twenty-five or more degrees hotter than outside the vehicle. Every year hundreds of pets die from being left in closed vehicles for just a few minutes. It's best not to leave Scout alone inside your car at all, but if you must, make sure the car is in the shade. The windows shouldn't be down so low that Scout could squeeze out, but they should be low enough on both sides to provide plenty of ventilation.

Veterinarians constantly patch up the tragedies caused by pets riding in the back of pick up trucks. Many dogs do it without mishap for years, until one abrupt stop or quick swerve tumbles them out on the highway. Dogs that ride inside the car with their head hanging out the window are also in danger. They often suffer serious eye injuries when hit at high speed by flying bugs.

Fall

Fall is a good time to take a stool sample to your veterinarian for a fecal exam and ask if any booster shots are recommended in your locale.

Temperatures can fluctuate rapidly during the fall, so be ready for sudden changes. It may be freezing cold for several days and then go up to 80 degrees for Indian summer. If it suddenly turns frigid and Scout is a house dog, put a sweater on him before a long walk.

Scout may start scratching soon after you start heating your house. This is usually caused by low humidity, which makes his outer layer of skin lose much of its moisture. Complications of dry skin are bacterial infections, which can be caused by Scout scratching and biting himself. A humidifier often helps prevent dry skin in dogs and humans.

Keep Scout away from the good-tasting, sweet-smelling, deadly antifreeze you put in your vehicles during the fall, and clean all spills completely. Just a little on the paws can kill a dog when he licks them clean. Signs of antifreeze poisoning are depression, lethargy, loss of coordination and liver failure.

While every dog deserves a Thanksgiving treat, too much turkey, turkey skin, mashed potatoes and rich gravy can give Scout a tummy ache or worse. You already know this, but your guests might need to be monitored. They may think you are depriving your poor pooch, but they aren't the ones who will be cleaning up the mess or paying the medical bill when the party is over. If some of your guests are children, and Scout eats gently from young hands, prepare for them beforehand by portion-packing a plastic bag full of the amount of goodies you know Scout can handle. Then allow your young visitors to feed Scout from the bag, either before or after you serve dinner.

Winter

Watch Scout's weight during the winter. His coat will grow thicker and may make him appear heavier, but underneath he may be losing weight. An active dog, especially an outside dog, needs to take in more calories during cold weather. Scout also

Carla Restivo's Sagebrush Tacoma Danni, TT, OFA, is in shape and ready for any weather. Here she gets ready to pull a sled.

needs as much fresh drinking water in the winter as he did in the summer. The dry, heated air in our homes causes water loss.

Purchase a warm sweater for Scout so he can be bundled up on frigid days, and you can both enjoy invigorating wintry walks. A canine coat may look more stylish than a sweater, but it seldom provides the underbelly protection that a bald-bellied Pit Bull appreciates.

Just as senior citizens mind the cold more than younger folks, so do senior dogs. And they can't decide to retire to Florida on their own. Keep your old dog's bed away from drafts, raised a little off the floor and cushioney soft. Younger dogs will enjoy the same treatment.

Dogs love to get close to a source of heat, but that can present several dangers. Although humans feel a spark on their skin immediately, a dog doesn't realize one has landed on it until it has burned through its hair and reached its skin. A cozy fireplace will be Scout's favorite winter resting place, so protect him by always having a fire screen in place. Even dogs that curl up next to wood-burning stoves must be treated for burns sometimes. The warmth feels wonderful and they may fall asleep too close to the stove, so use a fire screen there, too. Space heaters pose a triple threat. Dogs may chew the cord, burn themselves on the heater or knock the unit over and cause a fire.

Some Pit Bulls enjoy playing in the snow. Just provide water afterwards (snow is not a substitute for drinking water), take normal precautions against frostbite and watch for cracked pads or tiny cuts on the feet. If Scout is usually your couch companion, outdoor fun time should be introduced gradually and enjoyed in moderation.

If you have to leave Scout unattended in your car during the winter, don't shut all the windows no matter how cold it is outside. Scout still needs some ventilation, so open opposite windows about two inches.

The always-hazardous practice of allowing a dog to ride in the back of a pickup truck is most dangerous during the winter. Besides the potential for Scout to go flying in the event of a skid or an accident, winter adds the very real possibility of frostbite.

Walking in winter also has hazards, one of which is road salt. Road salt, unlike ordinary salt, can burn Scout's feet and mouth. Also, while walking he could kick it up onto his belly and burn himself there, too. Road sand, used mainly for traction, also contains chemicals for melting ice that can burn your dog. So keep a towel and an old throw rug by the door, and after a walk, towel Scout's chest, underbelly and feet, in that order. That will warm him and increase circulation, while getting rid of snow and chemical accumulations. It will also keep your floor clean and dry. If Scout's hair feels gritty, assume it is road salt or sand, and wash it off with warm water and a gentle pH-balanced dog shampoo.

Christmas cheer presents its own doggie dangers. Pretty poinsettia plants and merry mistletoe are both poisonous if chewed, and those glittery balls, so appealing to a playful Pit Bull, may be made of glass or easily shattered plastic. Every year dogs are shocked by mouthing the electric cords attached to Christmas tree lights and poisoned by getting into chocolate goodies (chocolate is fatal to some dogs). Reliably housebroken Scout may think the natural Christmas tree with its outdoorsy aroma made part of your home an appropriate potty spot, so be prepared with an immediate correction. If children are on your visitors list for Christmas dinner, prepare a portion for Scout the same as at Thanksgiving.

If Scout lives outside during the winter, he needs a well-insulated doghouse with deep, clean bedding and a main room free from drafts. Metal water dishes are taboo in winter, because he could get his tongue painfully stuck to the frozen metal. Constant access to fresh water is imperative, so if you are not able to frequently remove the ice from Scout's dish, consider self-warming water dishes.

It takes commitment and dedication to safely maintain a short-coated dog like the Pit Bull outside during the winter. Inviting Scout indoors is often easier, and surely more fun for both of you.

CHAPTER 9

What Can My American Pit Bull Terrier Do?

The American Pit Bull Terrier is suited for a variety of exciting activities and excels at just-for-fun games and at competitive events. But it has a serious side, too. Incredibly intelligent, though a mite stubborn at times, the Pit Bull is capable of winning some of dogdom's most stringently judged events. And the breed's gentle nature with people makes the Pit Bull an ideal candidate for animal-assisted therapy work.

FUN 'N GAMES

Because they are hardy dogs with high activity levels, Pit Bulls easily learn to play physical games. In fact, if you don't teach your dog to play a few games, it may create some and invite you to join in. Mental games are also fun for your Pit Bull and

American Pit Bull Terriers love games and love to learn, as demonstrated by Sarah Nugent's five generations of dogs, from fifteen-year-old Ch. Xpert Humes Topsy at left to two-year-old Our Gang's Little Nipper on the right. Four of the six dogs have obedience titles.

your family. They challenge your dog's memory and often make advanced training easier later on.

When playing with your Pit Bull, keep the mood light and enjoyable but always elect yourself, not it, team captain. No matter which one of you starts the game, you should be the one to end it. Call a halt when your Pit Bull is still engrossed in the fun and wants to continue playing. Games will lose their luster if you keep playing until it is exhausted or bored. It's also the captain's duty to call time out when the sport gets too rough or too wild. Provided you are consistent, your dog will soon learn to respect the rules of the game.

The games that follow are fun for puppies and adult dogs, and puppies as young as seven weeks old can start learning to play them. When roughhousing with a puppy, take its age, size and lack of coordination into consideration. Treat it like the robust little animal that it is, but don't overwhelm it with your physical superiority.

Puppies learn games quickly, but older dogs that haven't had the opportunity to play may take considerably longer to catch on. If your healthy adult Pit Bull isn't interested in playing games after a week or so of opportunities, don't despair. First, check your attitude. Perhaps you are trying too hard and making it look like work instead of fun. Next, check your timing. Was your dog full from dinner, or even sleeping, when you invited it to play? If a change of attitude or timing doesn't help, check the end of this section for tips on making playmates out of rug warmers.

Hide-and-Seek

Start playing hide-and-seek by putting your dog in a room and closing the door. Then hide a treat in a different room, just beside a table leg or partially under a chair, for example. Open the door, let your dog into the room and say "Find it!" in an excited voice. Of course your dog won't know what those words mean at first, so keep repeating them while encouraging it in the direction of the treat. Help your dog locate the goodie, but make sure it does the actual finding and picks it up from the floor, not your hand.

Now put your Pit Bull back in the other room and place another treat exactly where the first one was. Open the door, say "Find it" and watch what it does. You may have to help it find the treat a few times before it goes directly to it on its own. When it does, repeat it one more time and quit for the day.

Use the same hiding place on the second day and see if it takes the dog fewer tries to find it all by itself. When it immediately goes directly to the spot on the first try, it's time to start over with a new hiding place.

Don't tell your Pit Bull "No!" when it goes back to the original spot. It's learning to use its memory and that's good. In fact, once every so often have a treat waiting in the old hiding place(s) as well as the new one. Eventually your dog will learn to remember several rewarding locations. Continue adding hiding places as long as it keeps enjoying the game, and soon it will exercise its sense of smell as well as its memory.

You will probably invent many versions of this game. One variation that's fun for adult dogs uses the entire house, and your youngster does the hiding. Instead of saying "Find it," say "Find Bill." Meanwhile, Bill is hiding under the bed, or in a closet with the door slightly ajar, ready to give his dog a treat and a hug.

Besides being fun, games of hide-and-seek may enhance your Pit Bull's memory and scenting ability. Since food is the reward, play this type of game before feeding your dog its dinner.

Little League (or Maybe Major)

This game takes two or more humans and a ball that is too big for your dog to swallow. Tennis balls are just right for adult Pit Bulls, and something of similar weight, but somewhat smaller, will work with a puppy. Use the ball only for playing games. When playtime is over, put it away where your dog can't shred and swallow it.

To play this game, get your children or a friend to help, and roll the ball across the ground to each other with the dog in the middle trying to intercept. When the dog captures the ball, clap and cheer it on for a few seconds while it parades with its prize. Then say "Out," take the ball back and begin playing again. Later, you can advance to gently kicking the ball, and then to bouncing it across the ground. When your Pit Bull gets old enough and coordinated enough, try a real game of "Doggie in the Middle," being careful not to hit it in the eye with a hard pitch. No matter how mature your dog is, and no matter how good a ball player you are, remember to let it catch the ball every so often.

Some Pit Bulls don't want to give up the ball after they get it, and have to learn to respond to the word "Out." If your dog is willing to trade the ball for a treat, that's fine. But if it clamps down harder when you try to take the ball, drape your hand over the top of its muzzle, thumb on one side, fingers on the other, and curl its lip inward and upward into its large canine teeth while you say (not scream) the word "Out." Praise it when it lets go of the ball and resume playing the game.

If no other players are available, you can play a variation of this game by tossing the ball against a wall. Compete with your dog to catch it on the rebound, before or after the first bounce. As your dog becomes good at catching, start gently pitching a tennis ball (or lightweight rubber ball) underhand to it from a short distance, and encourage it to catch the ball before it hits the ground. Lengthen the distance gradually. Experiment to see what else your Pit Bull thinks is fun. Some dogs love to catch Frisbees. Others love to catch popcorn, one delicious kernel at a time. Your dog may enjoy all these games, plus others that you create especially for it.

Tug Without War

Pit Bulls naturally love games of tug, and many of them would be delighted to pull, shake and jerk their tug-toy long after you are exhausted. Hard rubber, figure-eight-shaped tugs and tug-toy balls attached to ropes are available at animal supply stores, or you can make a tug-toy out of scrap leather. Put tug-toys away after use, because it is extremely easy for a Pit Bull to tear these soft toys into a thousand pieces.

In your dog's mind, it is tugging to gain possession of the toy, so to keep it interested, let it win the toy sometimes. After the dog parades around with it for several seconds, make a few

You can channel your dog's love of tug-of-war into a fun game for both of you. Just remember, you have to win in the end.

obvious attempts to take the tug-toy from it. That will make it even prouder of its prize. Eventually call your dog to you, say "Out," and take the tug-toy from its mouth. (If your dog hasn't been taught to come when called, keep a long, lightweight leash on it during play sessions and use it, if necessary, to bring the dog to you.) At first, trade it a treat for the tug-toy. If it won't give up the toy that easily, use one of the methods described in the "Little League" section. A few dogs are so stubborn about keeping their prize that even those methods fail. If your dog is like that, put a drop of Bitter Apple on your finger and touch your finger to its tongue as you say "Out." Keep the Bitter Apple from touching the tug-toy, and as soon as your dog releases its grip, tell it "Take it" and play tug with it again.

Play as roughly as you want, as long as your dog responds to the "Out" command and never grabs at anything in your hand until it is told to "Take it." Remember, you are the captain, and your dog should always be aware of that. As long as you know you can stop the game at will, it's fine to intensify it by pushing your dog around with your hands and feet while it is tugging. That should make him growl up a storm, all in good fun.

Occasionally a dog becomes so excited playing the game that it grabs fingers by mistake, instead of the toy. If this happens to you, yell "No! Ouch!" (and maybe a few other things), and stop the game instantly. Put away the tug-toy and ignore your dog for several minutes; it will understand that it should have been more careful.

To speed up teaching "Out" and "Take it," sometimes practice them three times in a row before starting the game, and a time or two during the game. Then try to finish on a high note. For a great finale, let your Pit Bull capture the tug-toy, parade for applause and trade for a treat and a hug.

Fetch

Fetching (retrieving) games are favorites with an occasional Pit Bull, while many others couldn't care less. When tossing something for a young puppy to fetch, it's important that it see it leave your hand. If it brings it all the way back, trade it for a really special treat, like a tiny piece of cheese or burger.

Other puppies and dogs may chase the object, then parade it in triumph without bringing it back. If your Pit Bull is a parader, try putting it on a long leash before the game begins and gently reeling it in after it picks up the object. If it carries the object all the way in, give it a treat. If not, don't give it anything and don't be upset. You have a Pit Bull, not a Labrador Retriever, and this breed doesn't always have a strong retrieving instinct.

If your Pit Bull likes retrieving, the best way to keep it inspired is to never do too many retrieves at a time. Three in a row is plenty. After that, play tug as a reward.

Wrestling

Some people get a kick out of getting down on the floor and wrestling (or roughhousing) with their Pit Bull. They push or shake the dog, and the dog growls, takes an arm or leg in its mouth and pretend fights but never squeezes with its mouth.

Generations of Pit Bull owners have played this game with nary a mark on them, but they all understood that they were captain of the wrestling team, and their dog knew it, too. When wrestling, remember three things: You start the game. You stop the game (use the "Enough" command). And if your dog ever mouths you so hard it hurts, that not only ends the game, but everyone in the house should ignore the dog for the next half-hour.

The Pit Bull That Won't Play

Most dogs that won't play are adult dogs in a new home. Even though Pit Bulls change owners with more ease than most breeds, it may still take a few weeks until a new dog feels secure enough to enjoy games. Other adults may not play because no one ever played with them and they simply don't know how. This could be compounded if the dog grew up in a kennel without human socialization.

If you have a solemn dog, you're going to have to get silly before the dog will. Use especially interesting toys, like a rat made of fake fur or a bouncy latex hedgehog, and play with the toy yourself while your dog watches. Throw it and chase it (or enlist help from a spouse or child). Have an absolutely marvelous time playing with the toy, and occasionally tease the dog with it but don't give it to the dog. After two or three minutes of continuous (but not rowdy) fun, drop the toy near the dog and see if it picks it up. If the dog doesn't grab it immediately, pick it up and continue playing for another minute or two before putting the toy away until another day. If the dog does grab it, allow it to play with it itself for about thirty seconds, then gently trade it for a treat, play with it yourself and put it away. When taking the toy from your dog, do not use the "Out" command. You are simply developing its desire to play. Once the desire is there, you can start teaching the rules of the game.

CERTIFICATES AND SUCH

Dogs may earn certificates proving that they have sound temperament, acceptable social graces or fine conformation. These important programs, offered by various organizations, were all created to benefit dogs and their owners.

Certification Programs for All Dogs

Two noncompetitive certification programs test canine behavior in simulated everyday situations, such as a walk through the neighborhood or a visit to the park. While similar in structure, the two tests are quite different. The Temperament Test evaluates untrained responses to various stimuli, while the Canine Good Citizen Test evaluates learned behavior. Both programs help fight the ongoing battle against breed-specific and antidog legislation, so it is especially important that Pit Bulls participate in them. Also, both programs are available to all dogs, whether purebred or not.

Virginia Isaac's Pit Bull, Samson (right), earned his Canine Good Citizen title at the first such event held in California.

Qualifying for the TT

"A sound mind in a sound body," is the motto of the American Temperament Test Society (ATTS). Dogs that pass the ATTS's ten-part test earn a certificate, and their owners proudly display the letters TT (Temperament Tested) behind the dog's name.

In its flyer, the ATTS describes its test as follows:

> The ATTS test focuses on and measures different aspects of temperament such as stability, shyness, aggressiveness and friendliness as well as the dog's instinct for protectiveness toward its handler and/or self-preservation in the face of a threat. The test is designed for the betterment of all breeds of dogs and takes into consideration each breed's inherent tendencies.
>
> The test simulates a casual walk through the park or neighborhood where everyday life situations are encountered. During this walk, the dog experiences visual, auditory and tactile stimuli. Neutral, friendly and threatening situations are encountered, calling into play the dog's ability to distinguish between nonthreatening situations and those calling for watchful and protective reactions.

Your Pit Bull needs no special training or preparation to take the ATTS test. Well-socialized family dogs should have no trouble earning the highly respected TT.

For additional information and to find out where your Pit Bull can be tested, write the American Temperament Test Society, P.O. Box 397, Fenton, Missouri 63026. Request a flyer describing the test and a test schedule.

Qualifying for the CGC

"A Canine Good Citizen is a dog that makes its owner happy without making someone else unhappy," according to the American Kennel Club's Canine Good Citizen program booklet. That means Canine Good Citizens have learned to behave at home, are good neighbors and have social graces outside the home. Dogs that pass the ten-part test earn a certificate proclaiming them a Canine Good Citizen, and their owners proudly add the letters CGC to their dog's name.

The CGC test evaluates basic training (not formal obedience), so dogs are tested on how they behave during everyday situations such as meeting a friendly stranger, walking on a crowded street and meeting another dog while out for a stroll. Their ability to calm down on command following play, their reaction to distractions and their attitude when their handler is out of sight (separation anxiety) are also evaluated. In addition, they must obey simple commands such as "sit" and "down," but not with the precision of competitive obedience dogs.

Preparing for the CGC helps owners learn to control their dogs and makes the dogs more enjoyable pets. Many dog clubs and private obedience schools offer short courses in CGC training, and some of them use the test as their graduation exercise. In addition, the American Kennel Club offers free material to help people train their dogs for the test. Write The American Kennel Club, Attn: CGC, 5580 Centerview Drive, Suite 200, Raleigh, NC 27606. Ask for Canine Good Citizen training information and how to find a test near you.

Tests for American Staffordshire Terriers (and ADBA and UKC dogs)

Created and administered by the Federation for the American Staffordshire Terrier (FAST), the Social Compatibility Test (SCT) and the Conformation Evaluation are open only to American Staffordshire Terriers and American Pit Bull Terriers, both of which are considered American Staffordshire Terriers by the Federation. ADBA-, UKC- and AKC-registered dogs are all welcome to enter these noncompetitive tests, and dogs that pass are awarded certificates.

Social Compatibility Test (SCT)   FAST formulated the Social Compatibility Test to evaluate the distinctive temperament that should be displayed by the typical American Staffordshire Terrier. Dogs must pass the SCT before being considered for FAST's Conformation Evaluation, a requirement for a breeding dog.

The ten-part Social Compatibility Test evaluates dogs in simulated real-life situations including walking through a narrow passage with distractions on either side, being petted by several jovial people at once, being groomed by a stranger, reaction to loud noises and separation anxiety.

Conformation Evaluation   Dogs eligible for the Conformation Evaluation are examined one at a time by two evaluators and rated on how they compare to the breed standard. For this test, the standard has been divided into eight parts as follows: general impression, balance and size; head; body; running gear; symmetry, style and movement; tail; coat and color; and temperament. Emphasis is on athletic ability and soundness as well as physical beauty. Temperament is considered of prime importance, so dogs are not tested for conformation until they pass the Social Compatibility Test.

For information about the Social Compatibility Test or the Conformation Evaluation, contact FAST, Dr. Rudolph Kasni, 3 Yolanda Drive, Little Falls, NJ 07424.

Wonderful Work

A church calls its special volunteers Pets are Working Saints. Other groups have names such as Lend-a-Heart, Compassionate Canines and Sirius Angels. Who are they? They are just a few of the hundreds of volunteer groups made up of people who take their well-trained pets to nursing homes, therapy sessions for abused children, hospitals, rehabilitation centers, hospices for AIDS patients, cancer wards, schools for the physically or mentally challenged and even prisons.

Visits from friendly dogs cheer the depressed, entice elderly folks who usually refuse to leave their bed to get up and walk a dog and are one of the best motivators for children in need of physical therapy. True stories abound of tiny arms, unused for weeks, gradually reaching out toward a therapy dog, or mute four-year-olds finally whispering their first word—the therapy dog's name.

Dogs working in therapy situations are very special. They have to be completely confident and have temperaments stable enough to withstand hugs that are sometimes both too hard and too confining; petting that may look and feel much like hitting; and accidental bumps from equipment such as walkers and wheelchairs.

A thoroughly socialized, highly trained Pit Bull makes an ideal therapy dog, so if you want to lend some canine cheer to someone less fortunate, there are several ways to become involved in animal-assisted therapy. Some nursing homes develop their own programs, and you can volunteer with them directly. For example, a nursing home in New York has a pet visitation program complete with a detailed manual and stringent requirements. Besides passing the therapy version of the Canine Good Citizen Test (walkers, wheelchairs and other hospital equipment are used in the therapy version of the test), dogs must undergo a thorough veterinary examination, including stools and blood. Then four training sessions at the nursing home familiarize them with crowded elevators, slippery floors and the sights, smells and sounds of the institution. They also work with willing patients, first one-on-one, then in small groups of two or three and finally up to a maximum of six patients at once. As the dogs learn the institution's routine, they are evaluated by the staff. Those that pass the nursing home's strict requirements may serve internships of six visits within three months. If they do well, they are invited to a graduation ceremony and may sign up for regular visits.

At least two national organizations, Therapy Dogs International and Delta Society, have certification programs and tests for potential therapy dogs. They both require that dogs pass the therapy version of the Canine Good Citizen Test and, in addition, each organization has strict requirements of its own. For information on how your Pit Bull can become a therapy dog, contact Therapy Dogs International, (201) 543-0888 or the Delta Society, P.O. Box 1980, Renton, WA 98057, (206) 226-7357.

COMPETITIVE EVENTS

American Pit Bull Terriers excel at many competitive events and enjoy participating in them. Quick to learn and eager to please, they make top performers, provided their training is upbeat and creative.

Members of the Houston, Texas, chapter of Therapy Dogs International showing off their good manners. Photo by Sarah Nugent.

Samson comes over the top of an A-frame on an agility course.

Agility

Thrilling to participants and spectators, agility is the epitome of exciting teamwork. It blends desire, control, training and athletic ability into a rip-roaring good time. The object of the sport is for the handler to direct the dog over a timed obstacle course without the dog making a mistake such as touching a jump or missing a weave pole. Dogs jump colorful hurdles of various shapes and styles, hustle through tunnels, take a turn on the see-saw and hasten up and over ramps on courses that are never the same twice. Scoring is based on faults and time.

Agility training is a wonderful release for a Pit Bull's energy. It teaches dogs how to be under control and in high spirits at the same time, and turns dogs and owners into partners. The best place for you and your dog to learn agility is at a dog training school that is involved in the sport and has all the necessary equipment, or at an agility training club. Be certain the club or school has sturdy, safe equipment. Good instructors are upbeat and motivational, and their own dogs have earned agility titles. The best agility instructors keep the dogs interested and eager by using rewards such as toys, treats and praise.

American Pit Bull Terriers may participate in several different agility programs, all of which are fun and worthwhile. To learn about two popular programs and how you can participate, write or call: United Kennel Club, 100 East Kilgore Rd., Kalamazoo, MI 49001-5598, (616) 343-9020, or the United States Dog Agility Association, P.O. Box 850955, Richardson, TX 75085-0955, (214) 231-9700.

Obedience

Obedience training is a great outlet for a Pit Bull's enthusiasm and spirit. The sport encourages a dog to use its multitude of talents by making demands on its intelligence, trainability, memory and dexterity. It also stimulates its inborn desire to please by teaching it how to please you, and educates it in self-control without dimming its inner sparkle.

The best way for your Pit Bull to learn to obey, despite such distractions as strangers and other dogs, is to attend obedience school. Classes may be offered by dog clubs or by private instructors, and may be advertised in the yellow pages or the newspaper. Sometimes you will have to shop around[md]not for a bargain, but for the best school for you and your Pit Bull. Good obedience instructors do more than just call out commands. They offer alternative training methods when necessary, take the time to solve individual problems, constantly encourage the use of praise and are not prejudiced against any breed.

When you see how quickly your Pit Bull takes to training, you may decide to compete for obedience titles. Your American Pit Bull Terrier will compete in United Kennel Club (UKC) obedience, so discuss this with the instructor before joining a class. Although the class may be geared toward American Kennel Club (AKC) competition, the requirements for earning AKC and UKC titles are so similar that most instructors are willing to prepare students for competition in either organization. The three levels of titles offered by UKC are United Companion Dog (U-CD), United Companion Dog Excellent (U-CDX) and United Utility Dog (U-UD). If your instructor is willing but doesn't know the regulations for earning UKC obedience titles, write to the UKC, 100 East Kilgore Rd., Kalamazoo, MI 49001-5598, and ask for the obedience regulations.

Earning awards in obedience competition with their American Pit Bull Terriers are Lyssa Noble (left) and Candace Eggert (right).

Whether or not you compete in obedience trials, schooling gives your Pit Bull direction and stability. Learning to be attentive to you, heel smartly by your side, come immediately when called and reliably obey a variety of commands makes it a more agreeable companion. Use encouraging, creative methods, combine firmness with fairness and incorporate fun and games into every lesson, and you will end up with more than a well-trained Pit Bull. You and your dog will be a team.

Dog Shows (Conformation)

American Pit Bull Terriers may compete in shows held by clubs that are affiliated with either the American Dog Breeder's Association (ADBA) or the United Kennel Club (UKC). In fact, some dogs have successful show records in both organizations.

Dogs competing in conformation are judged on how closely their physical attributes conform to the written standard of excellence for their breed. So, in any given class, the winner of the class should be the dog that most resembles the ideal APBT described in the breed standard, second place should be the next closest dog and so on.

PORTRAIT OF A PERFORMING PIT BULL

Spartan's Samson, CD, U-CD, U-CDX, TT, CGC, Ag. I, II and Challenge, was a therapy dog, played flyball, pulled a cart, performed Utility, Schutzhund and basic Search and Rescue work, jumped a high jump with a raw egg in his mouth, carried his owner's groceries into the house and carried her purse in public places. For eleven years he traveled with his owner-trainer, Virginia Isaac, doing demonstrations in a five-state area.

When a member of congress tried to pass a breed-specific law against American Pit Bull Terriers, a TV talk show host invited Isaac to debate the congressman on live television. Isaac brought Samson along, and he was such a sensation that people all over California wired flowers to him and sent him cards. Best of all, the program was instrumental in stopping the proposed legislation. After that, Samson and Isaac appeared on numerous live television shows, doing their part to prevent breed-specific legislation wherever it threatened. They also visited nursing homes, where Samson's comical spirit gave pizzazz to every performance.

Samson does his stuff, whether it's agility, carting, obedience, or search and rescue.

Dog shows are actually elimination contests where dogs begin by competing in a class against dogs of the same sex and similar age. Next, class winners compete against each other and, finally, the top male and the top female of the day compete. Dogs receive points each time they win their class. When a dog accumulates one hundred points and meets its organization's other criteria, it is awarded a certificate proclaiming it a Champion, and the letters Ch. are added to the beginning of its name.

Champions compete against other champions to win the esteemed Grand Champion title.

If you believe your Pit Bull conforms so closely to the standard that it could be a show dog, begin learning how to win that championship by going to your first show as a spectator. That way you will learn the judging procedure. While procedure may differ slightly under different judges, there will be more similarities than differences, and knowing what to expect will be mighty helpful the first time you and your dog enter the showring.

Your dog should also know what to expect, so check the yellow pages or the newspaper for conformation classes, or ask your veterinarian if he or she knows where show training is available. If the training class you join is based on AKC conformation shows instead of UKC or ADBA, don't worry. Ring procedure is similar everywhere. Basically, your dog (on a lead) has to stand still in show pose (four feet squarely on the ground, head proud and tail relaxed) while being examined by a judge; allow its teeth (and testicles if it is a male) to be inspected; and gait (trot) beside you, smartly and straight, in the pattern requested by the judge. Most winning dogs have learned to show themselves to their best advantage despite the close proximity of other dogs, so training classes are almost a necessity.

If you decide to show your dog, consider it both a hobby and a learning experience. Always try to recognize the good points the judge found in the winner. Also, keep in mind that different judges may evaluate the same dog differently, and dogs have good days and bad days just like people. Today's loser is often tomorrow's winner, so if you are new to the sport, enter your dog in more than two or three shows to get a true picture of its quality. If your dog is a youngster, perhaps all it needs is a conditioning program and more time to mature.

Spayed and neutered dogs may not be shown in conformation. Also, male dogs having only one or neither testicle, and blind, deaf or lame dogs are not permitted to compete.

To find out where UKC or ADBA dog shows are being held, subscribe to the UKC's magazine, *Bloodlines*, or the ADBA's

Robinson's Bob Marley, owned by Mike Bell, demonstrates the weight pulling form that earned him the ADBA title Ace of Ace.

magazine, *Pit Bull Gazette*. Both advertise upcoming shows affiliated with their own organization. UKC's address is on page 184. Write to ADBA at Box 1771, Salt Lake City, UT 84110.

Weight Pulling

Would you like a legitimate way to show off your Pit Bull's strength, determination, courage and competitive spirit? Weight pulling competition could be the answer. At these demanding contests, extraordinary strength isn't all it takes to win. It also takes heart, tenacity and desire, that famous gameness of old.

When weight pulling, your Pit Bull will wear a padded harness fitted to its measurements. It should be at least one year old before beginning the sport, and trained to walk beside you, stay in place on command and come when called. Your dog will also have to get used to an object, attached about eight feet behind his harness, dragging along behind him. An excellent object to start with is a car tire lying flat on the ground.

Put a collar and leash on your dog so you can guide it to pull straight during training, but be careful never to jerk the leash so as to move both your dog and the weight. Dogs are required to pull off-lead at competitive weight pulls, so the final decision on how hard it will work will always belong to your dog. When training, keep in mind that a Pit Bull that is forced to pull never competes with the vigor of one that learned the sport through enthusiastic praise and reward.

Once your dog pulls the tire easily and straight, you can very gradually increase the weight by attaching a board to the top of the tire and laying weights on it. Because of friction from the grass or bumpy ground, your dog may already be pulling hundreds of pounds more than the actual weight of the tire, so be extremely cautious when you add weight. Three or four training sessions a week are enough, and the sessions should never be long. Two or three pulls of around twenty-five feet each are plenty, and each good pull should be wildly praised. To ensure a successful end to every practice session, reduce the weight for the final pull. Canine athletes have good and bad days just like human athletes. No matter how frustrated you may become, remember that weight pulling contests are won by confident dogs that enjoy the sport.

At most competitive pulls, a weighted cart must be pulled a distance of sixteen feet, and the time limit for each pull is one minute. The American Dog Breeders Association (ADBA) holds competitive weight pulls open only to American Pit Bull Terriers. It awards the title of Ace, and the esteemed Ace of Ace title, based on a point system. Write to the ADBA at box 1771, Salt Lake City, UT 84110, for a copy of their weight pull rules.

It's a good idea to watch a weight pull before entering. The ADBA's magazine, *Pit Bull Gazette,* has a show calendar listing upcoming shows that offer weight pulls. Detailed articles on preparing your dog for competitive weight pulls often appear in the *Gazette*, and in FAST's publication, *Fast Forward.*

Schutzhund

Created in Germany to judge the working abilities of German Shepherd dogs, the sport of Schutzhund (SchH) soon became popular with other breeds, such as Rottweilers and Doberman Pinschers. In the United States, many American Pit Bull Terriers have been successful Schutzhund competitors, even though the jump height of thirty-nine inches is meant for a taller dog.

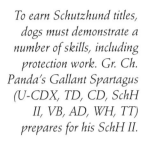

To earn Schutzhund titles, dogs must demonstrate a number of skills, including protection work. Gr. Ch. Panda's Gallant Spartagus (U-CDX, TD, CD, SchH II, VB, AD, WH, TT) prepares for his SchH II.

Schutzhund work makes demands on the best qualities of the American Pit Bull Terrier—courage, intelligence, confidence, dexterity, trainability, scenting ability and, above all, a sound temperament. When working toward a beginning Schutzhund title such as the "B," the concentration is on obedience and temperament. SchH I, II and III are novice through advanced degrees and involve obedience, protection (such as defending the handler in a prescribed way) and tracking tests (following a scent) of increasing difficulty. To earn a title, the dog is required to qualify in each portion of the test on the same day.

Dogs trained in Schutzhund are not attack dogs, but well-controlled, trained athletes competing at a disciplined sport. One component of the protection segment is an agitator wearing a special protective sleeve. Schutzhund dogs may look fierce when they attack that sleeve, but they treat it like a rousing game of tug and release it immediately on their handler's command. Also, the dogs are trained to attack sleeves, not people, and are even friendly to the agitator as soon as he removes the sleeve.

Taught and performed properly, Schutzhund work enhances the capabilities of an intelligent, trainable dog of sound temperament. Improperly taught, it is downright dangerous. Never answer an ad for guard dog or protection training in the mistaken notion that it will be competitive Schutzhund. Instead, contact the Federation for the American Staffordshire Terrier (FAST), or your local kennel club, German Shepherd club or Rottweiler club to locate a highly regarded Schutzhund instructor in your area.

There are a few national Schutzhund organizations, and although their rules differ slightly, their basic concepts remain the same. Trials held by FAST are affiliated with SchH USA and FAST's publication, *Fast Forward*, often runs articles helpful to those interested in Schutzhund. To contact, write FAST, c/o Dr. Rudolph Kasni, 3 Yolanda Dr., Little Falls, NJ 07424.

CHAPTER TEN

To Breed or Not to Breed

Excellence in dog breeding combines science, art, responsibility and a little luck, and there is only one good reason to bother with this time-consuming chore at all. That reason is a strong desire to improve the breed. The desire to produce better dogs than either outstanding parent should be powerful enough to make you study genetics, intense enough to make you memorize pedigrees, mighty enough to make you spend money and compelling enough to thrill you in spite of its considerable cost in time, effort and money.

Breeding is an exciting hobby, but it isn't for someone who is looking for the maximum return from a minimum investment. The world doesn't need more mediocre dogs of any breed, as there aren't nearly enough homes for the unwanted dogs that are already in shelters. Preserving the finest attributes of the American Pit Bull Terrier while trying to improve it means starting with the best and breeding to the best. That's why it takes time, study, effort and money.

Breeding also isn't for the faint of heart. Sometimes things go wrong. For example, an adored female may die giving birth,

The decision to bring puppies into the world is one that should be taken seriously. It's a demanding, costly and sometimes heartbreaking endeavor. These ten-day-old Old Family Rednose pups were bred by Dan Gibson. Photo by Dan Gibson.

leaving the puppies to be hand-raised. Or a middle-of-the-night emergency may bring unexpected veterinary bills.

If you have only a casual interest in breeding your female Pit Bull—perhaps to get back your investment in her, or to let your children see the miracle of birth—do yourself, your children and your dog a favor and leave the breeding to the professionals. The puppies could cost you more money than they earn, and, if something goes wrong during the delivery, your children may witness the spectacle of death.

SPAYING AND NEUTERING FOR A HEALTHIER, HAPPIER DOG

If neither dog breeding nor showing in conformation is your game, the nicest thing you can do for yourself, your family and your Pit Bull is to have it spayed or neutered. Females spayed before their first season, usually at around six months of age, are at much less risk of developing breast cancer than unspayed females. Because spaying removes the female's reproductive organs, spayed females never suffer cancers or infections of the ovaries or uterus. In addition, they don't have unwanted pregnancies and won't bleed all over your rug for several days twice a year.

Spayed females are also nicer to live with. They won't entice males to sing in chorus on your front lawn, and they won't suddenly develop a desire to roam. Spaying helps a female's disposition remain consistent, and lets her take part in competitive performance events, such as obedience or weight pulling, without a three-week break every six months. In short, spaying a female when she is young gives her a healthier life, gives you fewer hassles and doesn't add to the pet overpopulation problem.

Keeping your pet male dog intact for breeding purposes, either because you believe you are being kind to him or because someone with a female may seek him out for stud service, also does your dog and you an injustice. Neutering a male dog before he is a year old could save him the pain of prostrate problems, including cancer, when he ages. It will also make him easier to live with.

Male hormones make dogs desire every female in season whose scent wafts by on the wind, and some of them break doors, windows and fences to find the female. Male hormones also make dogs more aggressive toward other dogs and are sometimes implicated in housebreaking problems, such as scent marking (when the male lifts his leg and urinates on objects inside the home to stake out his territory). Frustration (caused by male hormones) is what makes a dog embarrass its owner by making love to the boss's leg during a dinner party. While neutering won't immediately cure a frustrated, dog-aggressive, escape artist with a housebreaking problem, it eliminates the production of male hormones and almost always starts him on the road to improvement.

Myths, Lies and Cartoons

It is a myth that spaying or neutering makes a dog fat and lazy. Overfeeding and lack of exercise do that. In fact, spayed and neutered pets are often the best performers in obedience, agility and other competitive events. Neutered males can consistently keep their mind on their work, and spayed females can compete throughout the year without losing six to eight weeks because of being in season.

Nearly all service dogs (guide dogs for the blind, hearing dogs, and dogs that help the physically handicapped) are spayed or neutered.

It is a lie that neutered males don't make good guardians. Not only will they fiercely protect their home and family, but they concentrate on their job better then males that have the scent of a female on their mind. Spayed females are also reliable guardians.

Cartoonists and comedians often get laughs by implying that male dogs think as humans do and are sad or resentful over being "castrated." While such skits are funny at the comedy club, the concept is absolutely ridiculous in real life. Dogs don't have human feelings about romantic love and sex. Dogs don't miss the hormones that made them feel frustrated and drove them to get into trouble. In fact, after they are neutered, most dogs become closer to their family. And that's where dogs really want to be.

THE FEMALE HEAT CYCLE

Unspayed female Pit Bulls usually come into season (heat) twice a year at roughly six-month intervals. They start when they are between six and twelve months old and continue all their lives. The heat usually lasts from eighteen to twenty-one days, and its first sign is a noticeable swelling of the vulva, following by bleeding (showing color). Males are often attracted to a female at this early stage, but she usually wants nothing to do with them and either sits down when they try to mount her, or fights them off. After seven to nine days, the bloody discharge changes to cream- or straw-colored, signaling the second stage of heat. The female's attitude often changes, too, and she may become friendly and inviting toward males. It is during this

CAN YOU SELECT THE RIGHT STUD DOG?

You have a female Pit Bull that is good in every way, except she is considered slightly small for the breed. You would like her to have puppies that will be medium-sized at maturity, and you're torn between two good stud dogs. Should you breed her to an excellent dog that is considered exceptionally large for the breed, or to an equally fine dog that is medium-sized?

In dog breeding, a small dog mated to a large dog doesn't make medium dogs. Instead, it makes some dogs that are too small and some that are too big. Breeding your small female with a medium-sized dog is your best bet. It should produce some dogs that are too small and some that are just right.

stage, which usually lasts from the tenth to the fifteenth day, that the female is ovulating and can become pregnant. The final stage of heat often continues until the twenty-first day or even longer. During this period the female is still attractive to males, but she usually wants nothing more to do with them.

When a female is in season, it's impossible to be too careful. Not every female's cycle or behavior is average, and some may be agreeable to breeding much earlier or much later than the norm. Since males are attracted to your door from the first swelling of the vulva until nature washes the scent of season from your yard, it's important to keep your female securely confined during her entire heat cycle. Females in heat have made escapes that the great Houdini would admire, and male dogs will do whatever it takes to woo your girl, including digging under and climbing over the fence.

If you bred your female on purpose, it's still necessary to confine her. Female dogs can give birth to puppies from two or more sires in one litter. You may have bred Nell to the best Pit Bull you could find, but if Bobbie Boxer climbed your fence, some of Nell's puppies may be pure Pit Bulls while others may be mongrels, or Pit Boxers if you must.

SEXUAL CHARACTERISTICS OF THE MALE

From the time a male Pit Bull is around eight months old until he is too old to stand, he will probably be willing to breed a female in heat. But stud dogs should never be expected to "perform" outside on hot, muggy days, because even if they succeed, they may still fail. Extreme heat kills sperm, so it's best to keep a stud dog in the shade, or even in air-conditioning, for several hours before he is used, as well as during the actual mating.

Although Pit Bulls of both sexes should be certified clear of hereditary defects before they are used for breeding, a defect called orchidism is seen only in the male and can be easily detected by the owner. Orchidism means the dog's testicle(s) did not descend into the scrotum. It is called cryptorchidism

---

Are You Ready to Be a Good Breeder (or Stud Dog Owner)?

- A good breeder starts with a female of high quality and excellent temperament, and assesses how well she stacks up to the ideal as described in the American Pit Bull Terrier standards. No dog is perfect, and a good breeder recognizes his own dog's strengths and weaknesses.
- A good breeder studies genetics.
- A good breeder analyzes his Pit Bull's pedigree before selecting (or accepting) a breeding partner.
- A good breeder makes a point of seeing several of her dog's close relatives as an aid to learning the strengths and weaknesses that run in the family.
- A good breeder selects a stud dog by pedigree, conformation and temperament.
- A good breeder has his Pit Bull tested for heredity defects (such as hip dysplasia) and sexually transmitted diseases (such as brucellosis) before the breeding, and demands the same of the opposite sex.
- A good breeder is a student of American Pit Bull Terrier history, so as to fully understand the traits she is trying to preserve.

- A good breeder has read widely on selective breeding, genetics, whelping and rearing puppies.
- A good breeder has watched or helped with the whelping of at least two litters before breeding his own female.
- A good breeder has her female examined by a veterinarian before she is bred, and knows the vet's availability in case of emergency.
- A good breeder has a breeder friend who will hurry over at any hour if moral support or help is needed during the whelping. A good breeder also expects to return the favor.
- A good breeder never breeds until he has a list of several reliable, caring people, each anxiously waiting to acquire a puppy from the breeding.
- A good breeder knows that breeding dogs is seldom a money-making venture and has put money aside so that unplanned veterinary expenses, such as an emergency caesarean, will not be a hardship on the family.
- A good breeder has the facilities to whelp puppies and the space and time to keep the litter healthy, exercised and socialized until they all have good homes.
- A good breeder is prepared to take back a puppy that doesn't work out.
- A good breeder knows how to raise orphan puppies.
- A good breeder has made arrangements with a dependable person who is willing and capable of taking over in the event of a family emergency or the breeder's own illness.

To sum it up: A good breeder has prepared the best possible mating and is prepared to handle the worst possible timing, health problems and finances.

It's a lot of work and considerable expense, but an excellent breeding program is worth it. Few thrills compare to seeing a puppy you planned grow up to be a beloved companion or successful show or performance dog.

when it affects both testicles, and monorchidism when it affects one. Some dogs with orchidism are capable of fathering puppies, but they should never be allowed to do so as they often pass the defect to their young. In fact, dogs with this defect should always be neutered because the undescended testicle(s) tend to become cancerous.

If you have a young male puppy with undescended testicles, don't panic too soon. Sometimes puppies' testicles do not fully descend until the dog reaches four to five months of age. Also, when the testicles begin to descend, one or both of them may appear one day and disappear the next, only to emerge for good a few days later.

BECOMING A BREEDER

You've been bitten by the dog show bug, have seriously studied the American Pit Bull Terrier and its standards and own one or two fine females. Now you have a definite goal in mind. There's a picture in your head of what the ideal Pit Bull should look like, and you believe that by breeding your best female to a carefully selected stud dog, you can produce the dog you visualize in your dreams. You're on the right track. Or maybe your excellent male with the impressive pedigree has won at a several dog shows. Now owners of some fine females have asked if he is available for stud service. You're on the right track, too.

For those with energy, enthusiasm and a never-say-die attitude, breeding can have many rewards. But the decision to breed a female, or offer a male at stud, should never be taken lightly. Anyone can mate two dogs, and any two dogs—even two mongrels that roam the neighborhood—can breed. But their irresponsible owners don't deserve to be called breeders. In good breeding, quality and care is the key. The checklist beginning on page 198 will help you determine whether you are ready to be a good breeder.

PUPPIES ON THE WAY

You bred Chita to a fabulous stud dog whose conformation and pedigree complement hers, and checked off the weeks on the calendar. You've gradually increased her food and divided it into two feedings. If your veterinarian recommended calcium or vitamin supplementation, you offered it diligently. The whelping

Zack and Brutus, two five-week-old pups bred by Candace Eggert, give the photographer the raspberry.

box has been ready for weeks. Now sixty-one days have passed, Chita is huge and you wonder if you should stay up with her all night every night until the puppies are born. Yes, you should be there in case she needs you during the delivery, but there are several signs that will usually (but not always) tell you when her time is near.

Two to three days before the puppies are born, Chita's hard, barrel-shaped abdomen will start to sag. She may lose her appetite or become finicky. Her breasts will get bigger and may be red, and the slightest squeeze may produce milk. She may sleep so soundly that she doesn't hear you open a box of dog treats, then awaken restless and dog your every footstep. A drop in her body temperature is the surest sign that Chita is within twelve hours or so of delivering puppies. Normal temperature for a dog is between 101 and 102 degrees, so a temperature under 101 degrees signals a drop. Chita may shiver due to either the drop in temperature or the turmoil inside her, but the shivering should stop after the first puppy is born.

As her time gets closer, Chita will scratch and paw at her bedding to make a nest, and may frantically remake the nest several

A brand-new litter! Cheryl and Jeff Helton's new mama, Ch. 'PR' Gaff's CA Hurricane Justice.

times. Be sure her whelping box is in a warm, draft-free place, and put many layers of spread-out newspapers in it. Later, as each puppy is born and the papers become wet and soiled, the top layers can be removed, leaving a clean bed for the next puppy. Also, be sure Chita remains in her whelping box. As females get close to whelping time, they sometimes become restless and start looking for other places to give birth. There are many stories of people arriving home to find their Pit Bull contentedly nursing her newborns on the waterbed or the sofa.

When labor begins, Chita will pant and you will see her stomach and flanks contract. The contractions may continue for a few minutes and then stop for a while, and this pattern may be repeated several times before the first puppy is born. Chita may strain, grunt, look questioningly at her tail end, stand up with her back arched, position herself as if passing a stool or lay calmly on her side. Labor isn't easy, but it shouldn't be agonizing either. Some bitches let out a yelp as their first puppy is born, and that is normal. But if Chita is screaming in pain with any frequency, call your veterinarian.

PUPPY DAY (OR NIGHT)

A wide, wet bubble at the vulva is the first sign that Chita will be a mom within minutes. If she is standing or swinging her tail end, be prepared to catch a slippery puppy. If she is laying down, or sitting on one hip, consider yourself lucky.

Some of Chita's puppies may be born head first and others rear first; both positions are just fine. Each puppy will emerge encased in a watery sac made of membranes (unless the pressure of being born breaks the sac, resulting in a dry birth, which is rarer, but usually also okay). Chita should remove the membrane from the newborn with her teeth, sever the umbilical cord from the afterbirth (placenta) and lick the puppy clean, stimulating it with licks and gentle pushes until it cries at least once and moves. Some Pit Bulls remove the membrane and stimulate the puppy before severing the cord, and that order of events is also fine.

If Chita doesn't do her job, you have to do it for her or the puppy will drown in its own fluid. First, tear the membrane from the newborn's face and head. Next, using a clean, soft towel, wipe the liquid from the mouth and nose. Now towel-dry the tiny body firmly enough to stimulate the puppy to breathe and cry.

Tear the umbilical cord last, because that part is no emergency. To sever the cord, first push the blood in the cord toward the pup. Next, tear the cord with your fingernails or a dull instrument, leaving an inch or a little more attached to the puppy. Don't use a sharp knife or scissors, as a clean cut bleeds more than a ragged one. If the puppy bleeds more than a few big droplets, tie the end of the cord with white thread, or put some styptic powder on it. While you are working on the puppy, Chita may decide she wants it back. Get it breathing and moving before giving it back to her, and perhaps she will take care of the umbilical cord.

Following the birth of each pup, Chita should pass an afterbirth, and following the afterbirth, some greenish liquid will flow out of her. Chita will probably want to eat the afterbirth, and that is just fine. The liverlike placenta is full of hormones that will stimulate Chita's maternal instincts, help her make milk and reduce her uterus to its normal size after all the puppies are whelped.

It's important to count the afterbirths. There should be one for each puppy, and it may be passed right with the puppy or right before the following puppy. The important part is that it is passed. Chita may or may not eat all of the afterbirths, but all of them have to come out. Retained placentas can lead to all kinds of problems that you and Chita don't need, so if you aren't sure of your placenta count, tell your veterinarian.

Most mama dogs rest between having puppies, and a couple of puppies may already be nursing lustily as the next puppy is being born. Twenty minutes to half an hour is the usual rest time for Pit Bulls, but Chita may keep you waiting an hour or two between puppies. As long as she isn't straining hard or often to no avail, everything is probably just fine. Things could also speed up, and Chita may give birth so quickly that she can't clean one puppy properly before another comes along. If that happens, help her with her motherly chores.

LIFESAVING SWING

Occasionally a puppy will have trouble breathing and if you hold it to your ear you may hear fluid gurgling. That means the puppy swallowed or inhaled fluid from the sac. You may be able to save such a puppy by holding it by the body with its head hanging straight down. Of course the puppy will be slippery, so be very careful not to drop it. With both hands holding the puppy, raise your arms, spread your legs, and swing the puppy down between your legs, being careful not to let it hit the floor. Some fluid may land on the floor while more may bubble out of the puppy's nose. Wipe the nose with a clean towel, and hold the puppy up to your ear again. If you still hear a gurgle, swing the puppy as before and check again. It may take a few swings to get rid of all the fluid that kept the puppy from breathing normally. When it appears to breathe easily, give it back to its dam.

WHEN WHELPING IS ALMOST OVER

When Chita relaxes, curls around her puppies, and nuzzles them proudly, it usually means all of them have been whelped. By now she may appreciate a snack of broth, ice cream or warm skimmed milk. It's also fine to offer Chita a little broth or skimmed milk between whelping puppies, but many dams refuse food or drink until labor is over.

After Chita rests a few minutes with her puppies, she should be taken out of the box so she can relieve herself (expect dark diarrhea) while the box is cleaned and made up with fresh bedding. She may not want to go, and might have to be forced to go out on a leash. Before allowing her to return to the box, use a warm, damp towel to wipe her clean. Work fast, as being away from her puppies will make Chita very nervous.

Once Chita has settled down with her puppies again, offer her a small dinner of boiled rice and cooked hamburger. Some new dams don't want to eat after having puppies and need the special temptation. Discuss with your veterinarian whether Chita should be fed vitamin, mineral and calcium supplements, and whether she should have an oxytocin shot following whelping (to help clean the uterus and remove retained placentas).

Another essential to discuss with your veterinarian is a vaccination and worming schedule for your new puppies. Prevention of deadly diseases should start early, and continue as often as your vet recommends.

SERIOUS SYMPTOMS

If Chita gets a condition called eclampsia (milk fever) she will become extremely nervous, stop caring for or nursing her puppies, tremble violently, run a fever and even walk strangely as her muscles become rigid. *This is an emergency*. Chita needs treatment immediately or she will die. Your veterinarian will give her a massive dose of calcium gluconate intravenously, and she will

ARE THE PUPPIES WARM ENOUGH?

Newborn puppies need warmth. In fact, a chilled puppy can't even digest its dinner and will soon die. How can you tell if your puppies are comfortable, or if you need to make their box warmer or cooler? Just see how they sleep.

Chilly puppies sleep piled up on top of each other. Hot puppies sleep spread out all over the box. Comfortable puppies sleep side by side; touching, but not huddled together.

If your puppies are chilly, a heat lamp or even a two hundred-watt bulb can be used to warm part of the whelping box. Place any heat source so it affects only half the box. Then the puppies can squirm toward and away from the heat as needed.

soon be herself again. Dogs that get eclampsia usually come down with it during whelping, or within the first three weeks of nursing.

Mastitis is another dangerous condition. Its symptoms are hard, hot, caked, sore teats. Usually only one or two teats suffer the condition while the other teats continue to function just fine. Don't let puppies nurse from the infected teats, and get veterinary help for Chita. She needs treatment with antibiotics to get well.

Unfortunately, there are several conditions and diseases that can attack a new dam and her puppies. If something doesn't seem right, don't wait to see what will happen. Instead, see your veterinarian.

SEE HOW THEY GROW

Healthy newborns sleep about 90 percent of the time and spend the rest of the time eating. But don't expect them to lie still, because sleeping puppies often jerk their limbs and bodies. This active sleep exercises their muscles and is a sign of good health.

Another sign of good health is strong suckling, finding a nipple quickly and hanging on as if glued to it.

From birth to three weeks, Chita will provide nutrition and do all the dirty work. With her tongue, she will stimulate each puppy to go potty and then clean up the results. Enjoy. You'll have enough to do later.

Puppies are born blind and deaf, with eyes and ears tightly shut. Their eyes begin to open when they are between ten and fifteen days old, and their ears start working a few days after their eyes open. Baby teeth, needle-sharp and temporary, emerge at the age of two or three weeks. They will be replaced by permanent teeth gradually, starting when the puppies are around four months old. Start clipping the puppies' needle-sharp toenails when they are around two weeks old, and repeat the process every seven to ten days. Chita will appreciate it.

Socialization begins with the breeder. When the puppies are three weeks old, they will begin recognizing and enjoying humans. Give them lots of individual attention by holding, petting and talking to them one at a time. When they are four weeks old, take each puppy away from the rest of the litter for around ten minutes a day at least four times a week. Increase the time and the frequency as the puppies get older, and arrange for them to meet both men, women and gentle children.

DETERMINING SEX

Ancient kings may have had their queens beheaded for not giving birth to a male heir, but modern science guarantees that sperm, not eggs, determine the sex of the young. In dogs, that means the male is totally responsible for making each puppy a male or a female. However, the female is responsible for the number of pups.

How do you determine the sex of newborn pups? Turn them over and look at their bellies. Male puppies have a little penis just behind the umbilical cord, while female puppies have a tiny vulva between their rear legs.

THE OTHER MOTHER—THE BREEDER'S ROLE IN SOCIALIZING THE LITTER

The first human a puppy sees when it opens its tiny eyes to a hazy, out-of-focus world is almost always the breeder or a member of the breeder's family. Through its sense of touch, it already recognizes the breeder's hands, and its developing sense of smell and hearing add to the familiarity. If the puppy has licked or suckled the breeder's finger, it will also recall the taste. Next to its dam and litter-mates, the puppy is most aware of the tall creature who alternately smells of soap, garlic, perfume and pizza. In fact, through interactions with its two-legged mom or dad, the puppy will establish its first opinion of the human species.

Gentle handling by the breeder will not hurt even very young Pit Bull puppies, provided the breeder has clean hands and has not been around strange dogs. Some breeders caress their puppies' backs and roll them over for soft, index finger chest rubs as soon as the umbili-cal cord heals. While it isn't good to spend hours stroking newborns, a few minutes a day per puppy gets socialization off to an early start.

It's great fun to sit on the floor and let your perky puppies test their legs by crawling all over you, and it happens to be good for their mental and physical development, too. But in addition to play-ing with the whole litter together, remember to single out individu-als. Every Pit Bull needs its very own few minutes of interaction with a person—one-on-one—in a different place, away from its litter-mates. That's when the puppy begins building confidence and devel-oping a personality all its own.

Studies by animal behaviorists have shown that all puppies go through critical periods of social development from birth to sixteen

Early socialization, under the watchful eye of the breeder or owner, is wonderful for young puppies, provided their vaccinations are up to date. Candy's Panda Bear, owned by Cathy Cleveland, already seems to believe the world is her domain.

weeks, and one of the most vital periods is between three to seven weeks. If a puppy lacks attention and mental stimulation during that period, it's doubtful that its personality and character will ever develop to its full potential

Between the ages of three to five weeks, all the socialization a puppy needs is four or ten minutes alone with a friendly person about four times a week. Five-week-old puppies need about fifteen minutes of individual attention four times a week and it's best if the same person doesn't play with them each time. Puppies should learn that men and women and gentle young people all make good friends. But keep it within the family and a few favored friends. Until your puppies have been protected by inoculations, they shouldn't be around unfamiliar people or dogs.

During individual socialization periods, condition your Pit Bull puppies to feel different textures under their feet. When the weather is nice, take a puppy outside and play with it on the grass. Then let it stand on concrete, provided it isn't too hot for tender pads. Rugs, tile, linoleum and wood all add variety.

When you are particularly busy and find it difficult to give the puppies the attention they need, take one puppy on your lap every time you watch television or read a book.

A few easily accessible (and free) toys can change your boring puppy room into a stimulating kindergarten. Plastic gallon jugs or half-gallon empty milk containers with the caps removed make wonderful puppy toys. When your litter gains the courage to approach and examine the bulky objects, each puppy discovers that it is able to dominate the lightweight plastic by dragging it around at will—a wonderful confidence booster. Cardboard boxes with holes cut in strategic places so puppies can crawl in, out and through also make fine temporary additions to the puppies' play area. Of course plastic and cardboard are not a desirable puppy diet, so if your youngsters want to swallow instead of just drag, shake and rip, they should be supervised during playtime.

It's important that your puppies become accustomed to household noise, and better still if happy associations are connected with some sounds. The place to begin is the most pleasant association of all: the food dish. Use metal bowls, and instead of laying the tins down carefully, allow them to rattle and clang a little.

The purpose of introducing various sights, sounds and textures is to familiarize your puppies with them gradually, not to frighten them. There is no need to become overly creative. Just use ordinary household activities and keep it simple.

Learning to eat is a sticky procedure, especially when you dive right in. These four-week-old puppies will be cleaned up by their owners, Cheryl and Jeff Helton. After puppies begin eating real food, most dams go on strike when it comes to clean-up.

WEANING GRADUALLY

There are several good puppy formula mixes available. Just mix the powder with water according to label directions, heat to lukewarm and serve. Begin offering the mixture to your puppies when they are three weeks old. A heavy pie pan makes a fine bowl for a medium-sized litter. With a large litter, use two pie pans or a big, heavy skillet.

Most puppies need a little encouragement to try lapping liquid instead of suckling, so gently dip each puppy's mouth into the mixture once or twice. After puppies taste it they usually want more, although many of them don't do too well on their first couple of tries. Have a couple of warm, damp washcloths ready to clean up your sticky puppies. Besides getting their heads completely covered in formula, some of them may go wading in the pan.

The puppies should live with Chita and continue to suckle until they are six weeks old, but the breast milk should be supplemented with formula from three weeks on. Feed formula twice a day until the pups are four weeks old, three times a day during their fourth week, and four times a day from five weeks old until weaning is complete. When the puppies are between

DOG BREEDING TERMINOLOGY

Almost every hobby has a language all its own. Whether or not you want to become a breeder, knowing the meaning of the following words and phrases will help you communicate with breeders.

- *Bitch*—Proper terminology for a female dog.
- *Brood bitch*—A female dog used for breeding.
- *Culling*—This difficult, but necessary, part of selective breeding involves painlessly eliminating malformed, sickly puppies and those with undesirable traits. Generally, the better the breeding pair, the less need for culling.
- *Dam*—Mother of puppies.
- *Genetics*—The science of heredity. It deals with how physical and mental traits are transmitted from parents to offspring.
- *Gestation period*—The approximately nine-week period from the breeding until the whelping. It varies between sixty-one and sixty-five days, with sixty-three being average.
- *Get*—The puppies sired by a particular stud dog or whelped by a particular bitch.
- *Gyp*—Slang for a female dog in some sections of the country.
- *Inbreeding*—The mating of closely related dogs, such as father to daughter, son to mother or full brother to full sister. Breeders debate the values and dangers of inbreeding. While some insist that it produces defective dogs, others argue that inbreeding doesn't create defects, it simply makes them show up so they may be culled, which ultimately strengthens the strain. While knowledgeable, professional breeders use inbreeding to intensify desirable traits and establish a strong strain of excellent quality, this practice is not recommended for new breeders.
- *Like begets like*—The earliest form of selective breeding. Long ago, the various breeds of dogs were established this way. Breeders selected similar dogs of the type they were trying to establish, bred them and discarded any puppies that did not closely resemble the parents. Today, "like begets like" is still one of the most important principles of genetics.
- *Line*—A family or strain of related dogs.
- *Linebreeding*—A safer form of keeping it in the family, and the base of many of the finest breeding programs, linebreeding is the mating of more distant relatives, such as uncle to niece and grandsire to granddaughter. A long-term breeding program, linebreeding produces consistent quality (without as much danger from

(continued)

defects as inbreeding), providing that the parents and their ancestors were all excellent specimens. When the breeding program consistently emphasizes one particularly admirable ancestor, it is referred to as backcrossing.

- *Litter*—The puppies of one whelping. In Pit Bulls, four to eight puppies is a normal-sized litter. Less than that is a small litter and more than that is a large litter.
- *Outcrossing*—While outcrossing really means mating dogs that are unrelated, most dogs of the same breed are related in some way if you research back far enough. In breeder's terms, outcrossing refers to mating dogs that have no common ancestor for five or more generations, or are from completely different lines. Breeders generally outcross for a particular reason, such as getting puppies with bigger bones or better heads, but outcrossing is always a gamble. Along with the desirable traits may come unwanted traits, so breeders should study the potential partners and their pedigrees well before arranging an outcross.
- *Prepotency*—The ability of a dog or bitch to give many of its traits to its offspring. This is extremely important in an animal selected for breeding. Although inherited traits could be good or bad, when a breeding animal is said to be prepotent, it almost always means that he or she transmits desirable traits.
- *Selective breeding*—Breeding the best to the best by studying pedigrees and accessing conformation and temperament.
- *Sire*—A male dog that has fathered (sired) puppies.
- *Stud dog*—A male dog used for breeding.
- *Stud fee*—The amount charged for the services of a stud dog.
- *Wean*—the process of teaching the puppies to eat and drink from a bowl instead of from their dam's teat. Weaning should begin at around three weeks, and be complete between six and sevenweeks.
- *Whelp*—To give birth. Also, a puppy is sometimes referred to as a whelp.
- *Whelping box*—A comfortable wooden box or a pen for the bitch to whelp her puppies. A whelping box should be in a warm place with no drafts, and be big enough so the bitch can stretch out with a few inches to spare. The bottom should be raised a couple of inches off the chilly floor and heavily padded with soft washable or disposable material. Most Pit Bulls are very careful of their precious puppies, but could accidentally crush a puppy against the wall during their sleep. That's why the best whelping boxes have a guard rail. The rail should be on all four sides, about three to four inches from the bottom and three inches from the sides of the box. The whelping box is usually home to the dam and puppies for three to four weeks.

four and five weeks old, begin softening a good quality commercial puppy food in the formula before each feeding. Between five and six weeks old, separate the puppies from Chita during the day, but allow them to spend the night together. When they are six weeks old weaning should be complete. Don't be surprised if Chita is delighted to be removed from her duties.

LETTING GO LIGHTLY

Letting your puppies go to the loving homes you so carefully selected can be both a heartache and a relief. Think of it as a beginning rather than an ending, and let the new owners know that you will always care about their puppy. Along with the papers, the health record and the feeding schedule, give them your friendship. Tell them to call you if they have questions, and ask them to show you their pup at six months and at a year, or send photos if they live far away. The relationship between a caring breeder and a responsible new owner could be the beginning of a rewarding, lifelong friendship.